The Enterprise of the Future

How companies develop through the pioneer, differentiated, integrated and associative phases.

Moral intuition in leadership and the organisation development

Friedrich Glasl

Translated by Christian von Arnim

Foreword by Professor Daniel T. Jones

Hawthorn Press

Publisher's Note: This work is based on two lectures which were delivered by the author at events organised by the publisher Freies Geistesleben in Autumn 1993 and Spring 1994. This was to mark the occasion of the 100th anniversary of the publication of Rudolf Steiner's *Philosophy of Freedom*. The author revised the lectures for publication.

The Enterprise of the Future: Moral Intuition in leadership and organisation development

German edition *Das Unternehmen der Zukunft*
© 1994 Freies Geistesleben, Stuttgart, Germany

English edition Copyright © 1997 Hawthorn Press
Published by Hawthorn Press, Hawthorn House,
Lansdown Lane, Stroud, GL5 1BJ, United Kingdom

Translated from the German by Christian von Arnim
Cover picture by Ivon Oates
Typeset in Plantin by Frances Fineran at Hawthorn Press
Printed by Redwood Books, Wiltshire

British Library Cataloguing in Publication Data applied for

ISBN 1 869 890 79 5

Contents

Foreword *Daniel T. Jones* v

Part I: The enterprise of the future

Introduction 3

The four phases of the developing
organisation: an overview 5

The developing enterprise more
closely observed: the pioneer phase 17

The differentiated phase 21

The special features of the integration phase 25

The characteristics of the associative phase 31

The four phases of the developing organisation
and the evolution of human consciousness 39

New problems call for new abilities! 45

Part II: Moral intuition in organisational development and leadership

The contemporary relevance of
the *Philosophy of Freedom* 53

Belief in progress in 1894 and 1994 55

The contemporary relevance of epistemology 59

Practical application of epistemology in
organisational consultancy work 67

The hubris of constructivism 73

The ego-less individual 81

Moral intuition 85

The potential for conflict in communities 89

Free morality assumes maturity 95

The way through the labyrinth 101

References 105

Foreword

Professor Daniel T. Jones, Cardiff University Business School

The significance of the first of these two lectures is that Fritz Glasl has taken Bernard Lievegoed's three phase model of organisation development on to a fourth stage, reflecting the challenges as we reach the end of the century. His fourth, associative phase also connects with the vision Rudolf Steiner had 75 years ago of the associative economy and with the current awareness of the environmental consequences of economic activity.

Fritz was one of Lievegoed's closest collaborators and first presented this fourth phase in a thoroughly revised and co-authored version of Lievegoed's path breaking book, *The Developing Organisation,* originally published in 1969.[1] Lievegoed's insight that the phases in the development of the human being was itself an archetype for the development of organisations proved to be way ahead of its time. While the biological metaphor is now widely used in management thinking, Lievegoed's pioneering work is still not fully appreciated in the English speaking world.

As the traditional assumptions of management thinking have crumbled, managers are searching for ways of making sense of the challenges they face. Glasl shows how this four phase model is helpful in diagnosing the challenges facing an individual organisation – allowing one to choose the type of change appropriate to the circumstances of the organisation

---

1. Friedrich Glasl and Bernard Lievegoed, *Dynamische Unternehmensentwicklung,* Verlag Freies Geistesleben, Stuttgart, 1993.

and to link changes at the different levels of the organisation – in vision and leadership, in social relationships and in the operation of the core processes. He also illustrates some of the other diagnostic tools he uses in working with some of the leading firms in Germany, Austria and Switzerland, as well as with schools and government departments.

This model also allows us to understand the evolution of management thinking and practice over this century. It is no accident that our own model of craft production, mass production and lean production closely mirrors the first three phases of the Lievegoed/Glasl model.[2] While there are always new pioneer firms and firms maturing into the second phase in the economy, there is also a dominant form of management exhibited by the leading firms of the day – the craftsmen entrepreneurs of the industrial revolution, the Ford motor company through to the post war American multi-nationals and more recently Toyota, Honda and Sony.

The idea of the organisation as a big machine reached the limits of its usefulness in the 1980s, when scale and specialisation were taken to their logical conclusions. At that time the world was full of firms that had lost sight of their customers and whose employees and suppliers had resorted to protecting their own islands of activity in a bureaucratic nightmare – classic late second phase symptoms. Several of the routes proposed as solutions turned out to be blind alleys.

The engineers' dream of extending the mechanical paradigm to its limits – the firm with no people, and lights out factories full of robots and computers – now lies in tatters as dust gathers on monster machines that never paid back their capital costs or delivered the promised flexibility. The natural response from labour to this vision, particularly in Germany and Sweden, was to try to protect jobs in islands of autonomy free from management control. Unfortunately autonomous work groups without a clear objective did not

Foreword

turn out to be more fulfilling and the groups themselves lost sight of the overall purpose of the enterprise, to meet customer needs at a realistic price.

During the 1980s leading Japanese firms gave us another perspective, that refocused economic activities on *customer value* and organised the whole *value stream* from raw materials to end customer as a continuous flow, from which all non value-creating activities were gradually squeezed through the collaboration of employees in teams and firms with their suppliers.[3] It challenged the notion that the health of the economic system was achieved by every firm optimising its own behaviour in an atomistic struggle for survival. Instead it became evident that only if all the firms involved in creating a product or service worked together would customer needs be met most efficiently and with the minimum waste of resources and human capabilities.

Glasl's fourth phase extends this concept of the value stream to encompass the whole network of stakeholders with whom a firm interacts and 'shares a destiny'. The Unipart Group, one of the real pioneers of the stakeholding philosophy in the UK, defines this as its employees, its shareholders, its customers, its suppliers and the communities in which it trades. Glasl calls this a 'biotope', which emphasises the holistic interdependence of all the elements within it, necessary for the health of the customers, the employees, the enterprises, the economy and the environment. Above all the healthy organisation of such a 'biotope' involves a broadening of consciousness by each

---

2. James P. Womack, Daniel T. Jones and Daniel Roos, *The Machine that Changed the World*, Rawson Macmillan, New York, 1990.
3. James P. Womack and Daniel T. Jones, *Lean Thinking*, Simon & Schuster, New York, 1996.

participant to take into account the needs of all the elements within it. Our concept of a collaboration of the key firms linked across a value stream, which we call a *lean enterprise,* is a practical step in this direction. One can already see the beginning of such collaboration between firms in many different industries.

The significance of the second lecture is that it challenges the theoretical underpinnings of the relatively new science studying whole systems, stemming from neurobiology and computer science, such as systems dynamics, chaos and complexity theory. This has been welcomed as a holistic alternative to the reductionist paradigm of studying the behaviour of ever smaller atoms and sub-nuclei. It focuses instead on the relationships within the total system and the networks and patterns that arise out of their complex interaction. The fascination of this approach is visually captured by the stunning pictures generated by the Mandelbrot set. It also appeals to new age thinkers seeking a spiritual dimension to this work.[4]

Glasl welcomes the holistic perspective but challenges the logical conclusions derived from it. He warns of the dangers of unquestioning acceptance of this approach, whose apparently benign and democratic promises are not borne out by its own logic. Indeed he shows how this logic leads to a denial of an independent spiritual existence, a denial that knowledge of the truth is possible and that there is any basis for making decisions based on morality. He warns that the conclusion leads to the justification of the use of force against other human beings and the earth, and ultimately to totalitarianism.

---

4. This work is usefully summarised by Fritjof Capra's book *The Web of Life,* Harper Collins, New York, 1996.

Foreword

He contrasts this directly with Rudolf Steiner's holistic image of the developing human being and our ability through independent thought and intuition to acquire knowledge of the right thing to do. In this age, where most business leaders and organisations are having to make enormous transitions to new ways of working together and with their partners in their 'biotope', the ability to collectively form a picture of the right way forward and to overcome conflict is one of the greatest challenges of our time.

There are no text book solutions any more – solutions have to be lived into and not prescribed. Reading this profoundly challenging book several times will provide real nourishment to those struggling at this most important frontier of human experience.

Hereford
February 1997

PART I

The enterprise of the future

How companies develop through the pioneer, differentiated, integrated and associative phases

Introduction

The Enterprise of the Future is a challenging topic for a management consultant working with and studying organisational development. After all, as a management consultant I am concerned with giving advice, not with an eye to the past, but with an eye to future tasks. Enabling an orientation towards the future is, in any case, the essence of consultancy work. I was happy to take on this subject in order to take a deeper look at the questions: What age are we living in? What is happening around us, with us and within us? What does that mean for the development of enterprises, of statutory organisations, of voluntary organisations such as churches and schools? What is happening here? What is required of people to ensure that they do justice to their work tasks and avoid producing out-of-date results? For example, do they try to avoid squeezing yesterday's solutions into a present-day form?

My view of the things which will face us in the coming years is one of profound structural change. What we observe in contemporary events such as the fall of the Berlin Wall, the opening of eastern Europe and the transformation of economic and political systems is only the beginning (see F.Glasl, 1992). I do not therefore share the optimistic view that after a short period of turbulence we will, in the near future, get back to a steady cruising speed at 35,000 feet. Moreover, I believe that the structural changes which we are now witnessing in Europe are connected with the tensions between East and West, between rich and poor, with the problems which we ourselves have contributed to causing – we and our parents' and grandparents' generation. And I believe that we are now reaping what was sown there. These structural changes mean that business, political, social and community leaders will no longer find much external support from stable conditions. Increasing chaos will mean that they will be subject to a kind of new test of fire and water. The decisive question will be whether they can find *inner* support, whether they can find their personal inner reference points in a turbulent world.

It will therefore be important to develop the capacity for self-orientation and self-direction for staff as well as people in leading positions. This personal reference point results in my having a vision that goes beyond the current uncertainties, in having insight into the new beginnings behind the surface turbulence and conflicts. These questions will be addressed in Part II which explores the importance of moral intuition for leadership and organisational development. This concerns anyone who is active in a creative way, whether in business, the arts or in the community.

Together with Bernard Lievegoed, I set out in the book *Dynamische Unternehmensentwicklung* (1993) how an organisation can develop through various stages. I will describe the key elements in this process of development of enterprises. Then I will focus on people, on what the phases of the developing organisation means for them and for human growth.

The four phases of the developing organisation: an overview

The four phases of the developing organisation will first be summarised. Then I will deal with them in greater detail. In order to understand the enterprise of the future, we need to picture its overall development so that we can recognise what has been created when a particular enterprise, school or hospital is founded. *(Figure 1)*

For the first, pioneer phase, I like to use the metaphor, 'The enterprise as brotherhood or family'. Look at what happens in families. It does not matter whether the mother or father is the dominant parent; look at the relationships, the way in which family life grows around individuals, the peculiarities, gifts and weakness of the individual family members. It is a structure with quite specific roles, ways of working and dealing with one another, which grow out of the individuals. Something similar also happens in the very first phase in the evolution of an organisation, which we have described as the pioneer phase.

The second phase, the 'differentiation phase' begins when the external or internal demands begin to change, so that a crisis occurs in the organisation. This raises the question: Is it possible to continue in this informal style, or do we need a different approach for managing the organisation? As a rule, something new occurs at this point. At first this happens without having been thought about and the organisation turns into a quite different entity. A rational approach and cool calculation become important. The enterprise is thought of and constructed as an apparatus, a mechanism: labour is divided as in a set of cogs in which nothing is left to chance.

Enterprise of the future

	2. Differentiated phase	3. Integrated phase	4. Associative phase
...as large family or tribe	The ent... mechar...	...as ...	The enterprise as distinctive part of the biotope or network
Personification to the point of personality cult, heroes, gods, sagas, legends	Mater... means of incorporation in the foreground, rituals	...hought ...loped ...olic culture, actions, material and personal symbols	Conscious cultivation of culture, cultural dialogue in the enterprise biotope

Figure 1: The metaphors of the four developmental phases (Glasl/Lievegoed 1993, p.124)

BIOTOPE
A small area, such as the bark of a tree, that supports its own distinctive community.
(ECOLOGY)

ECOLOGY
The study of the relationships between living organisms and their environment.

The four phases: an overview

The ways people are managed and work together, how customers, patients or students are treated, is organised exactly. The unspoken guiding principle behind this is the idea that the whole should function like a well-oiled machine, a mechanism. That is typical for the second phase, the 'differentiated phase'. Every last little part has its task, its role and everything should mesh, should function smoothly without any friction. Even the language which is often used in this second phase indicates that clearly. It is the sober language of engineers, not of biologists or family members.

The differentiated phase, too, encounters certain limits, because the enterprise threatens to drift apart. If an enterprise wants to both maintain its position in society and face up to future tasks, then it has to decide whether it wants to revert to the pioneering culture, expand it further and perfect it, or whether it has the courage and the ability to dare to take the next step into another type of thinking.

New paradigms, new concepts and guiding principles are required for the development of the 'integrated phase', the third developmental stage. Here, a kind of thinking which sees the organisation as a living organism needs to take over. It is a welcome development that in current management theory a break is finally being made with the narrow 'scientific' thinking which predominated in the 1960's and 1970's. This was characterised by mechanistic thinking in which a variety of statements was made about human beings or the social organism which used computers as their model. If you want to understand human thinking, it was often said, you really have to understand how a computer works. It is greatly to be welcomed that today modern management and organisation theory states: If we really want to make progress, we cannot draw conclusions about human beings or the social organism on the basis of an analogy with technology; on the contrary, we have to learn from the biological sciences.

What I was able to write in 1993 in the new edition of Lievegoed's book, was rejected as 'unscientific' some twenty years ago when Professor Lievegoed published *The Developing Organisation* (1974). At the time, Lievegoed was the subject of criticism by the experts in organisation theory: 'This is discrimination in favour of biology, you cannot do that. It is an anthropomorphic way of looking at social structures.' To be accused of bias in favour of biology was a severe criticism. If you read the current publications of the self-same authors who at that time raised accusations of discrimination in favour of biology, if you attend their lectures, they are now claiming that: 'The biological sciences hold the key! We have to learn from them!'

Characteristic:	Subsystem:
1. Identity	Cultural sub-system
2. Policy, strategy, programme	
3. Structure (organisational structure)	Social sub-system
4. People, groups, climate, management.	
5. Individual functions, organs	
6. Processes	Technical and instrumental sub-system
7. Physical resources and means	

Figure 2: The seven characteristics and the three sub-systems. (Glasl, Lievegoed 1993, p13.)

The four phases: an overview

With the step into the integrated phase, the breakthrough into other functional levels can only succeed if we break with mechanistic thinking. We need to allow ourselves to be guided by organic, living thinking in the way we develop management and organisational structures, relations with customers, school children, and patients. We need to understand that besides the technical processes there are many other realities which cannot be seen through engineering goggles. This means that I am missing the point if I try to understand all of reality simply by reaching out for the so-called 'facts'. If we want to do people full justice we have to realise that soul realities play a role as well as the hard facts. For what people mean, the images they have of reality, the awareness which they aim to develop – all of these things create social realities in an organisation.

The development of the third phase, the 'integrated phase', requires thinking in various sub-systems (see diagram). We have to learn to handle the demands of technology in the technical and instrumental sub-system. We have to understand the demands of the social system, the laws and developments which govern life in that sphere. And every enterprise has its cultural sub-system: its values and guiding ideas, its ways and patterns of thinking, its written and unwritten principles. All of these things are engaged in a trialogue. I cannot organise the whole enterprise on the basis of its technical principles. To do so, would be to cause the social element to degenerate and become deformed. That would result in sickness and all kinds of other things. But neither can I develop and manage it purely from a social point of view or a purely spiritual or cultural one. After all, in the final account the organisation is actively engaged in this world which is formed through the interaction of spirit, soul and matter. *(Figure 2)*

Enterprise of the future

1. Pioneer Phase

'Everything for our customers'

Customer loyalty, personal knowledge of the customer's situation

Personality of pioneer shapes structure, ways of working

Charismatic and authoritarian leadership

Functions organised around abilities of people.

Improvisation – flexibility

Means 'irrelevant to result'

Dangers:

Chaos, arbitrariness, lack of independence among staff

Figure 3: Main characteristics of the four development phases

The four phases: an overview

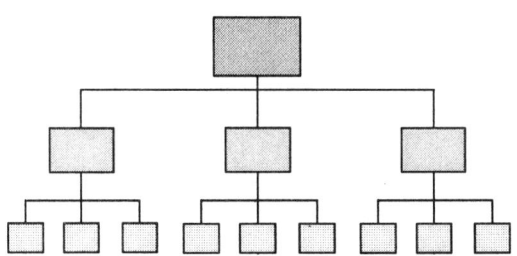

2. Differentiated phase

'We sell what's good for us!'

System, order, logic, control, feasibility

Formalised structures, regulations, standard rules

Functional structure, staffing structure

Differentiated management levels: planning, organising, directing

Management, business-like, rational.

Staff adapt to the given circumstances

Division of labour! Separation: of planning implementation – control

Dangers:

Over-organisation, over-formalisation, fragmentation, rigidification, bureaucracy

(continued)

Enterprise of the future

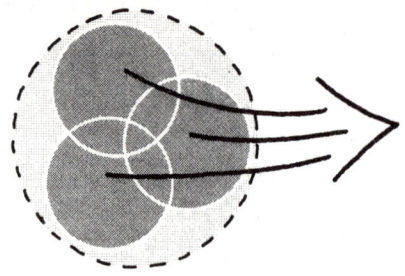

3. Integrated phase

'We solve customers' problems! We create customer benefit!'

Vision, targets, strategies, developing basic principles co-operatively

Interlinked, smaller, relatively independent units, entrepreneurial spirit

Situational and developmental management

Integrated functions, teams, autonomous groups

Self-planning, self-organisation, self-control

Dangers:

Tendency towards independence, insistence on autonomy, debates about aims and strategies for their own sake

Fig.3:(cont.) Main characteristics of the four development phases

The four phases: an overview

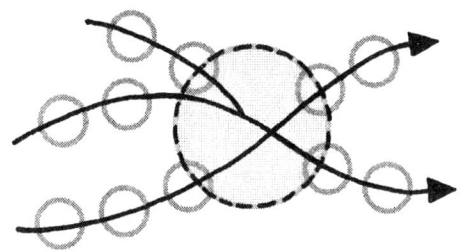

4. Associative phase

In biotope of enterprises: Shared destiny relationships

Relationships to other organisations, stakeholders and environments

Long-term policies, trust and cooperation

Structural incorporation of external bodies, many associative forms

Situational and developmental management, capacity for conflict

Integrational functions, interface management, autonomous teams, self-managing

Responsibility for, and management of processes far beyond limits of enterprise: suppliers, customers through to waste management

Dangers:

Power blocks through strategic alliances, state within the state

This is followed by a further stage of development, the fourth, 'associative' phase, which provokes widespread discussion. This is because another developmental threshold in the shaping of organisations needs to be crossed today. It is not only important to structure and manage one's own organisation well, but also much more is at stake! We have to recognise that our own organisation can only be successful if it sees itself as an element in a biotope, a whole inter-dependant network of relationships between different organisations and stakeholders.

This does not mean that 'my' organisation becomes subordinate and disappears, but that it is important how this entity relates to others in an ongoing network of co-operative relationships. So we do not buy something here or deliver something there on a one off basis, but we cultivate relationships with buyers, suppliers, consumers, the community, relationships which are more than the opportunistic exploitation of an opportunity. These are a 'shared destiny relationships' because an enterprise has to enter into a relationship with a variety of organisations in its environment; a relationship which is characterised by an attitude of responsibility, of a certain permanence, and which is based on continuous development. As the manager of an enterprise I cannot say: 'I'm all right Jack, even if my suppliers are going to the wall!' The formula for success could be defined in the following terms: I and my suppliers and distributors will do well if each one of us thinks not only of their own advantage, but as a matter of principle of our joint co-operative benefit. That sounds like idealistic dreaming far removed from reality. But the breakthroughs in modern organisations reveal precisely such developments leading to associative working.

The four phases: an overview

I have described the evolution of the four phases in broad outline. I will now fill in some of the detail of what has so far been presented in schematic form. (Figure 3)

The developing enterprise more closely observed: the pioneer phase

When we look at the basic principles of the pioneer phase we can say that the establishment of an enterprise or other organisation only has a chance of success if there is a real demand for the work which I believe I am competent to offer to customers or clients. My focus is on the customer, the patient, the school pupil, the citizen. Their needs and their problems are my problem. In the first phase I am strongly driven, therefore, by the needs of the customers. With this kind of approach, I reach a point in which the be-all end-all and is represented by the visionary element or, as it is also described in organisational behaviour, 'charismatic leadership.' The charisma, the particular gifts which I as founder have demonstrated, and which is recognised by the others who have embarked on the adventure of the new enterprise with me, is experienced and confirmed. This means that the various people who are working together in this pioneering organisation have a joint purpose because the pioneering leader has communicated to them the aims of their work and how they are to treat one another. That is also why I said that in this first phase the whole development of management and organisational structures is modelled on the family. The pioneering enterprise is person-centred in every respect.

If management consultants are unable to think in these evolutionary images they will enter a pioneer enterprise and give advice which is appropriate for the differentiated phase. Such consultants will say: 'The whole enterprise is completely disordered, illogical. Why is Mr Jones doing this

Enterprise of the future

while Mrs Smith is responsible for purchasing and customer service as well as a little bookkeeping. This is chaos, why such confusion?' One would have to answer: 'Take a closer look, take an interest in what people can do... look at the people, then you will understand why the tasks have been divided as they have been.'

Another key point is improvisation. The only really decisive element in the pioneer organisation is what I physically perceive as necessary. This perception intuitively guides my actions. I can well remember the time when I worked for several years in a printing and publishing house in Vienna. We had our Friday planning meetings at which we planned ahead with the aid of a magnetic board for the following week: How can we make the best use of the various printing machines so that the capacities of staff and machines are well utilised? We pushed the counters this way and that and then finally it all came together. At the end of the following week we would then check how things had really worked out. They were always completely different, unexpected, improvised and always better than what we had laid out in the plan! Through alert improvisation we always managed to make better use of the resources than through planning. That is the advantage of good improvisation. But it always assumes that people know one another, respect one another and are close to one another.

The weakness which can break such a pioneer enterprise and in a crisis can lead to its destruction, is this personal element – the tendency to develop a personality cult and personal dependence on the founding individuals. It may be a school with founding teachers who on the basis of their educational skills laid the successful foundation stone for the school. But ten or fifteen years later they may no longer be the people with a real sense of what is required. A new generation has emerged but the pioneers continue to insist

The pioneer phase

that they were the founding teachers and that they must continue to be followed. That simply does not work. In such a situation the pioneer group becomes a clique which is intolerant and cannot stand criticism and which has grown to believe that it must enforce respect. The result is a cult of the personality, and dependency. In reality the over-mature pioneer phase has turned into a 'theocracy' which denies others the right to independent thought! An enterprise which has reached such a stage of development is of course incapable of recognising, grasping and responding to continuously changing challenges. A crisis may rapidly develop which threatens the very existence of the organisation.

The differentiated phase

The step into the differentiated phase, where rational mechanistic thinking is the determining factor, means that I rely on logic for the next developmental stage. This is appropriate for this phase. I think about what goes where? Which people can perform what functions? How does one know the work which needs to be done even if one is not familiar with the abilities and backgrounds of all the staff? After all, I cannot always look in a person's file if I do not know from personal contact the knowledge and skills which he or she possesses. How can I penetrate the organisation with my thinking? How can I understand its logic?

An organisation can continue to grow when a certain order and logic are present. The result is, of course, that the things which were improvised formerly and could be thought up on the spur of the moment can no longer be left to chance or whim. Things have to be organised so that they can be anticipated, planned, controlled; they have to be fixed, formalised, standardised, certain rules and procedures have to be created. If that is done the publishing company, hospital or enterprise can grow qualitatively and quantitatively. It can take on more complex tasks because it makes use of the specialist knowledge of its staff. Specialisation – in contrast to the universalised skills of the pioneer phase – is very important in the differentiated phase and creates the opportunity for quite a different approach to problem solving. But specialisation entails, of course, that the things which are split up have to be brought together again at a later stage. The necessary counterpart to that is co-ordination through requisite regulations or mechanisms in the language appropriate to the concept of the enterprise as a mechanism. The division of labour – a necessity in contrast to the chaos

Enterprise of the future

of the pioneer phase – means: Who is good at planning? Who is good at implementation? Who would be most appropriate to take over bookkeeping, accounting or proof-reading, who could perform supervisory functions well? These are all specific skills. We divide and share them. And if the tasks become even more complex, we have to divide and differentiate further.

You can see that this represents a change, that a different climate rules which requires a change in attitude in order to achieve something positive. The dangers are as follows: If this division, this specialisation goes on unchecked, it can easily become one hundred and ten, one hundred and twenty percent. The work is divided into ever smaller units and it loses its wider context. If that occurs, the need for co-ordination inevitably grows. Who makes sure that such co-ordination is co-ordinated? The co-ordination co-ordinator. What happens then? Can anyone still retain oversight in such a situation? I have to formalise and regulate things to an ever greater extent if the whole business is not to dissolve into its constituent parts and develop a destructive dynamic of its own. Such formalisation ensures that our own form of expression, our own thought processes become increasingly important. And if we are not very careful we no longer pay attention to the customer but our attention is directed primarily inwards because staff begin to think only about how this could still be refined and that might still be perfected further, how this mechanism might be developed and how that control network be made watertight.

This internal orientation then leads to a pathological deformation, to so-called 'target inversion'. Just as we know about temperature inversions, there are also target inversions in organisations. They occur when it becomes more important that the work is done according to the regulations than that it is done properly for the customer. This then

The differentiated phase

becomes the key problem of the bureaucratic administrative enterprise (F. Glasl 1983, p.75).

Now, I have been asked to provide training in various European and non-European countries. I recall the first seminars in 1986 – at the start of perestroyka in the former Soviet Union – when I was working with the top managers of major Russian enterprises. These managers had command over some 30,000 to 60,000 people. They recognised themselves very well in the concepts of the differentiated phase since the whole of business thinking in the Soviet Union was characterised by mechanistic thinking. But the surrounding state and administrative system, the whole political system too, gave every indication of being mechanistic through and through and resting on such a way of thinking.

These top Soviet managers were extremely proud of it until they were forced to discover: 'It does a lot, but we fail completely to grasp certain aspects of reality with it!' It could be clearly experienced how the mindset of these people, who were of course trained in dialectical materialism through their higher education, began to creak because what they had possessed until then as the leading scientific way of thinking was shown by my work with them to possess certain shortcomings. They also said: 'We have noticed that we are stuck unless we begin to treat people on the basis of a quite different understanding. Mechanistic thinking does not actually bring us close to the real questions and problems.' What I described with the pioneer phase was certainly not worth discussing from their perspective because the process of establishing an enterprise was never such that something was allowed to grow, that people could find themselves. An enterprise was simply placed somewhere quite inappropriately from the drawing board of the organising authority, a decision dictated by raw materials and energy requirements. And there it was supposed to function from day one like a clock which has just been wound up. They too began to notice that something was wrong, that something had been overlooked.

The special features of the integrated phase

Progress into the third phase, with its different way of thinking, values and image of human beings and their work, requires fundamental change. The transition does not always take place smoothly. A struggle is involved. The development of an enterprise in the pioneer phase means blood, sweat, and tears, anger and quarrels, people are criticised and rejected, others can do nothing wrong... It is a psychological struggle. If these conflicts are not consciously tackled at the level of the cultural sub-system of an organisation, many conflicts arise.

The developmental step into the integrated phase means that I begin again at a basic level and ask: Why are we here? What is the basis of our existence? Who actually needs us? What purpose do we fulfil? And not: What do we want to off-load, what do we have in stock and want to get rid of, what makes a nice little earner? The guidelines of the integrated phase are: What does the customer really need? What are people concerned with today? We have to ask: What is the context, the environment, in which this organism or organisation has to be seen? What does that context demand? I have to look at the enterprise once more from the outside inwards.

Steps towards developing this phase always have to start at the non-material level: customer benefit, the values we want to live by, the real problems behind the immediate demands of people who make use of our services. Other people, management and staff have to recognise the necessity of entering a dialogue. What is not required is that someone presents himself as a pioneer and says this is our course of action, this is our product range, the next step is this! The decisive element at this stage is that the aims of the enterprise are supported by everyone, that it is a concern of leading staff members that they really put their lifeblood into it. I can no longer handle customer problems from a distance, I have to take on their concerns as things close to my heart. The modern specialist literature, which knows what it is talking about, is also increasingly using such language: 'Not only the head, but the heart too has to be addressed!' This means that I have to enter into dialogue with the workforce about middle-term planning, strategy and policy. I have to make an effort to ensure that the philosophy, the underpinning values, of the enterprise is formulated and carried by many people. If I do that, people will be able to act much more independently on that common philosophical basis; if everyone is involved, if a consensus exists I can allow people to work with a great deal of autonomy. I can describe spheres of action in global terms, I do not need to compose telephone book-sized job descriptions with immense detail: What are your tasks on page 1, page 2, etc., what is your area of responsibility? I do not need to do that. But I can build on people's inner understanding and they can respond more intelligently to the things which they see.

This means that the qualities demanded of managers in the integrated phase are quite different from the mechanistic orientation of the differentiated phase. The key things here are being able to support staff in such a way that visionary powers are awakened and activated in them as opposed to the 'greatest leader of all time' telling them what to do. The integrated phase should not be ruled by the orders of a single person, should not be dependent on a single charismatic figure, but all staff members should be enabled to develop and utilise their abilities.

But the other side of the coin is also important. Managers need in turn to have the honesty and truthfulness to ask:

The special features of the integrated phase

Does what we do correspond to what is needed? Can we critically think through what we do and evaluate it? Those are new management abilities.

The step can then be taken to a more integrated way of working in terms of how tasks and functions are defined. In other words, the step can be taken not only to areas where I myself am responsible for planning, organising and implementation to a greater degree, but also for controlling functions. So then I feel myself responsible for the way in which I co-ordinate my work with my fellow employees on either side. Thus the key qualities here are self-development, self-organisation, self-planning and controlling. These are the guiding principles of the integrated phase.

Every action is built on thinking which aspires to the consistent creation of values: What happens at every stage of the work process? What is my contribution to the final customer benefit of the readers of the books, the patients who want to be cured, etc.? These things apply just as much if I work in the laundry or am servicing the lift. What is my contribution to final customer benefits? That question should be alive in everyone, that is the quite different form of awareness informing the integrated phase.

Bernard Lievegoed's first description of the integrated phase more than 20 years ago was an original contribution to understanding the developing organisation. It is true to say that it has taken until now for managers to become mature enough to understand these ideas and to develop organisations on such a basis.

And then the discussion broke in the business world about lean production, lean management and the lean enterprise (see J. Womack, D. Jones, D. Roos 1991; F. Glasl, B. Lievegoed 1993; F. Glasl, E. Brugger 1994). Is it something ephemeral or does the concept lean enterprise, lean production, lean management hide something new?

Enterprise of the future

What is the idea behind it? Professor Daniel Jones from Cardiff University in Britain is one of the three authors of the world best seller *The Machine That Changed The World,* (1991). We had known one another for more than ten years and I was fortunate enough that he sent me the book fresh from the printers, before reviewers and readers became aware of it, with the invitation: If something comes of it, are you ready to undertake missionary work with me on the Continent?

My first question was, of course, does it contain anything new, are the ideas good or are they deceptive? Can they be welcomed from a more profound spiritual perspective? We spent a long time debating the issues, for much of what is contained in the term 'lean enterprise' has been practised in Japan for the last 20 years and is now filtering through to the West. There are many similarities with what Lievegoed described 20 years ago in his concept of integration: the emphasis on individual responsibility, personal development, the focus on customer benefit and on the value creation process. That is all realised in the concept 'lean'. But there are many things in these lean enterprises in Japan which go beyond the concept as described at the time by Lievegoed. A further paradigmatic transformation is involved which moves phase three into phase four of the developing organisation.

And this essentially creates the link with our central topic: 'What does the enterprise of the future look like?'

The boundaries of the integrated phase can be described as follows. In this phase we still think very much of our own organism – our school, company, organisation. We make use of what comes in via the suppliers and have the interests of our customers at heart. We are primarily market-oriented, customer-oriented. But there are things which go beyond that. It is precisely these things which I describe, extending Lievegoed's concept, as the associative phase in the fourth stages of the development of enterprises.

The special features of the integrated phase

The quintessential lean enterprise

Every action in the enterprise...

1. ...is consistently focused on optimum customer benefit within the context of the wider social benefit

2. ...is carried by an awareness in the people concerned for the whole of the value creation process beyond internal and external organisational barriers

3. ...rests in its internal and external relations on binding trust with a commitment towards the long-term common good of the associated and mutually dependent enterprises

4. ...is continuously focused on the economical, respectful and caring treatment of all resources (materials, space, equipment and auxiliary means, energy, time, people and environment)

5. ...builds on the awareness, responsibility, creativity and capacity for development of people and together with them endeavours constantly to achieve improvement and innovation,

   ...all of this on the basis of consistent guiding principles and values which are internally and externally equally valid.

Figure 4: The quintessential lean enterprise
From: Glasl, Brugger 1994, p.16 ff.

The characteristics of the associative phase

As it grows in maturity, we can never look at and handle what happens in an enterprise as if it were an island. On the contrary, our contribution to customer benefit is a small tributary in an all-encompassing flow of value creation. This stream of value creation started a long time before our enterprise and flows on after the contribution of our firm has been made. That is why we have to look 'upstream' to our suppliers and ask as a publisher, for example: What happens with the processing of the raw materials and semi-finished products which are supplied to us? How does the paper factory ahead of me work? Does it look after natural resources? What is happening? Can everything it does really be justified in terms of customer benefit? How does value creation or value destruction continue after me?

In other words, I place myself in a far larger context of the economic process than was the case in the integrated phase. I cannot get beyond a certain point with the thinking of the third phase, namely that it is sufficient if my enterprise is doing well. In the associative phase I have to think in the following terms: If the biotope, the whole interdependent economic, community and ecological network, is doing well because we are working for and with one another, then my enterprise will also prosper. If I am egocentric, then the others will also suffer. If as an automobile manufacturer I attempt to squeeze my suppliers beyond the margin of profitability, then I weaken the suppliers on whose effectiveness I depend. The stranglehold of the purchaser means that the supplier is no longer able to invest as much in development and training, the products become less

Enterprise of the future

innovative and quality suffers. After all, I weaken, destroy and squeeze dry the supplier, who should be my best friend, only for my own short-term enrichment. That will affect me as well. It is precisely with this kind of short term, company-centred thinking that the associative model makes a break.

The development towards the associative phase is closely connected with the question: How does the stream of value creation, of which I am only a modest part, flow – what happens before me, what happens after me? What is my place in that? To what extent do I take responsibility for what happens before me and after me? That is one of the key points. The successful lean enterprises in Japan have shown it by example for some time already. The best concrete examples of how it works in practice can be seen in Europe now too, beginning in Britain (see F. Glasl, E. Brugger 1994, p.76ff., p.111ff.). On the Continent there are also enterprises which are successfully struggling with the associative idea and where people are saying: 'Customer-orientation, market-orientation, that's fine. But I have to expand the idea of market-orientation, by saying as an automobile manufacturer that it is not only my problem how the trade, the wholesaler and retailer, deals with the car. It is also my problem what happens to the car after it has come to the end of its life. Is it being dumped in the countryside where it pollutes the groundwater as it rusts away somewhere, etc? This is also my problem as the managing director of Mercedes Benz, VW or BMW. What happens through to the scrapping of the car? This is an essential step in expanding responsibility for the whole process in relation to the customer and extremely important in the associative phase.

An example: I work as a consultant for the computer manufacturer Hewlett-Packard, whose German subsidiary has its headquarters in Böblingen. Some time ago I presented the four phase concept to the whole of the management

The characteristics of the associative phase

team. The most senior managers said: 'It is true that we cannot produce new computers until we can give a guarantee to people that what finally happens to the things when they are no longer working is also environmentally sound. If we take on this responsibility and act accordingly, then this is actually a success factor in our sales strategy if we really take responsibility for the disposal of the equipment.' 'If we do that,' concluded the Hewlett-Packard people, 'then we also have to ask what metals or substances are built by the suppliers into the circuit boards which we use in our equipment. If toxic substances and heavy metals are causing a problem at that stage already then we cannot shirk our responsibility. On the contrary, we have to start a dialogue with our suppliers because we have a responsibility here which we share with them. We cannot simply say: Solve the problem, but keep the costs down because we will squeeze you. Rather: If it is the case that responsibility does not end at the goods entrance of our company but continues further, much further, namely to the extraction of raw materials: Where does our supplier's product come from? What is destroyed when uranium is mined? Do people put their lives at risk, what happens to the landscape when we use uranium ores? If it is the case that we bear a responsibility when we look upstream in the process flow to its source, then we carry this responsibility together with our suppliers at all stages.'

In business, we really need to have 'salmon consciousness' and always swim back to the source in order to find out what is happening there. Under those circumstances we have to enter into a quite different relationship with our suppliers. Not that we should attack them and gobble them up. Simply to buy, buy, buy until a dinosaur is created is the least imaginative and fruitful way forward. It does not solve any problems. On the contrary, we have to grasp the challenge which says: 'How can we recognise the independence of all our suppliers, indeed, promote it, but in such a way that we grasp responsibility with them jointly in the flow of value creation? That means looking together with them at how they might produce and supply differently, or how they might prevent driving unnecessary miles which only pollute the air. How can the delivery of materials be organised so that assets are not destroyed?' That then leads to a great variety of forms of shared responsibility, from suppliers to raw material extraction and downstream to sales and the retailer, even as far as the final disposal of the product.

In presenting this concept with its wide-ranging responsibility for the whole process, from the source to the sea as it were, I have to emphasise the following. This organisational and management perspective has the aim of placing what happens in business back into the cycle of nature in a responsible manner, just as agriculture, for instance, has to be seen as part of the cycle of nature. I describe that as 'acting consciously in business starting from nature and back to nature'. In other words, as a single enterprise I create a quite different relationship to the planet earth than was the case previously.

To use Rudolf Steiner's words, (Steiner 1915), we experience the world in its totality and have to make that experience our responsibility. The earth as celestial body, as an organism, is in reality the body of Christ and everything that we do to it we do to that body. If we carry that awareness into our business behaviour then we have the opportunity to approach the challenges of the future in a substantially different way. I am now talking about the whole question of the environmental damage caused by business, by the wrong political decisions for example, as well as by mistaken consumer behaviour. The only chance to deal with these questions is for the concept of value creation to be extended as broadly as I have described. That, of course, represents an

The characteristics of the associative phase

enormous expansion of our awareness horizon and breaks out of the traditional framework of business ethics. We may be able to think and comprehend it, we may be able to grasp the whole epic business process to its full extent with its long pre and post-history – but do our actions already accord with it? How can we still improve our actions in order to begin to rise to the challenge or to become more aware of our social responsibility? That is the real key question facing the enterprise of the future.

I have presented these elements of the associative phase from the perspective of awareness and ethics. Let me indicate a few more points to clarify the concept of the associative phase as it has been touched upon in practical terms by the 'lean enterprise'. If I have acquired this kind of value concept and make value creation in such a comprehensive way the core element of my business activity, it has a further implication. It means that I can only do it – in concentrating on my own internal business affairs – if my business together with my suppliers and retailers has pledged that it will continue developing, that it does not simply want to remain stationary. My relationship is also a learning relationship with the suppliers and the retailers, a developmental relationship, a 'shared destiny relationship' as it is called by the lean enterprises in Japan (see F. Glasl, E. Brugger 1994, p.16ff). This destiny concept means that so-called lean enterprises spend approximately four times as much on training and staff development as traditional automobile manufacturers for example. Development – training – further education – staff development: these are continuous tasks jointly undertaken with those who supply me and who take my goods.

I have visited various enterprises in Britain which have been acting in accordance with these ideas for years, for example Nissan, Honda, Unipart and Airbus. They provide the evidence of the kind of money which businesses are prepared to invest today in skills and knowledge, in the human resources of their suppliers even if the benefit accrues to the suppliers at first. But this means, of course, that *if* it is my concern that they engage in continuous development because I as automobile manufacturer can then assume, for example, that the people there will be able to build technological advances more quickly and better into a catalytic converter, then this development of the supplier benefits everyone whom s/he supplies. The suppliers also know that this mutual pledge applies to everyone involved in the whole value creation process.

That is a very important paradigm for me, a guiding principle for the development of the fourth phase or associative phase. The basis of my consultancy work as well as my teaching and research work at the University of Salzburg is anthroposophy, the science of the spirit as introduced by Rudolf Steiner and as it has been further developed by Bernard Lievegoed, for example. I am convinced that the social forms which will occupy us intensively over the next decades already exist in embryonic form. The challenge is to develop the associative phase beyond the integrated phase in original forms other than presently practised in Japan. I am certain that the associative development of an enterprise – with customers, suppliers – is something which Rudolf Steiner already put forward as a vision for the development of the economy in the early years of the century: the associative economy.

Today I am myself surprised that I wrestled for so many years with the attempt to find the correct name for this developmental phase. What name should I give to this fourth child after the integrated phase? At first, in one of my first publications where I wrote about initial ideas for this fourth phase (F.Glasl 1975), I chose the description 'social phase' or 'macrosocial phase'. I was not satisfied with that and later it

The characteristics of the associative phase

suddenly occurred to me that what was emerging with this development was the embryonic form of what Rudolf Steiner describes as the associative economy. It is already being practised – only not here! But a start is being made. It is not something which is being prescribed as moral medicine by some head-in-the-clouds idealist with no idea about business: 'Be trusting and treat your suppliers nicely.' That is not what is happening; on the contrary, it has been demonstrated that this type of relationship of trust is also more sensible from an economic point of view. There is greater benefit for the customer and for society which has to deal with the economic and ecological issues. Greater benefit accrues and in the end there are fewer social costs due to waste disposal and other previously ignored side effects. The demands which we ought to make if we are acting on the basis of moral considerations are, furthermore, a sensible and wise option.

The four phases of the developing organisation and the evolution of human consciousness

I would like now to approach the question of the enterprise of the future from an even deeper level. What do we do as human beings, what happens to us when enterprises develop in this evolutionary way from one phase to the next? What demands are made of people in terms of their awareness and attitude?

In my view, the challenge facing people becomes clearest if we look at the evolution of the enterprise in four phases against the background of the development of human consciousness in its various phases as described by Rudolf Steiner.

Here, too, I build on ideas developed by Lievegoed and the NPI-Institute for Organisational Development which was founded in Zeist, Holland, 40 years ago. We can say, using the language of anthroposophy, that my spiritual attitude, the way in which I deal with people and work in the pioneer phase can only be understood if we use the expression 'sentient soul'. This is a human capacity which gives me direct sensory perception of the events around me. Georg Kühlewind describes this very aptly as 'participating consciousness'. I feel the world. I become immersed in something, in the world, and that is reflected in me as a sentient being. But it is reflected, it affects me, I am a part of the reality which I perceive. It is this *stance of the sentient soul* which provides the key to understanding community

Enterprise of the future

Evolution of human consciousness and of organisations

1. Sentient soul community	2. Intellectual and mind soul	3. Consciousness soul	4. Anticipation of spirit-self community forms
Direct perception, participating consciousness	Ordering of perception, interpretation, analysis comparison	Perception – interpretation – meaning / questioning meaning, meta-level	Organ of higher intelligence and wisdom
Classical family, tribal community	Sensible regulations, norms, systems	Target focus, insight, responsibility – autonomy – ego character	Common good – own good; destiny relationship – sympathy with fellow human beings → Christ
Closeness, sympathy (and antipathy)	Distance, power of antipathy	Consciousness – self-consciousness – meta-consciousness	
Warmth	Light, air	Water	Earth

Figure 5: Evolution and the stages of consciousness

Phases of the developing organisation

development in the *pioneer phase*. The pioneer phase, seen in families and tribal communities can be characterised in this way – like all archaic communities. Rudolf Steiner described this state of consciousness as underlying, as determining, the Egyptian-Chaldean cultural epoch. These archaic forms of community are then taken up again by a social organism. Just as past stages of development are echoed in embryology, so an enterprise too lives primarily in this sentient soul element from the time of its inception.

This sentient, charismatic or pioneer phase is developed to the full. Then, at some stage, the next move has to be made in order to meet the demands of customers, technology and the market. Then an attitude of soul becomes apparent in the next developmental phase which is characteristic for the *differentiated* phase. This is the *intellectual or mind soul*. Rudolf Steiner shows that this form of consciousness was developed in the Graeco-Roman cultural epoch. This soul mood has the effect that I not only approach things with the power of empathy and sympathy and but to a much greater extent with the power of antipathy. It means that I consciously create distance, that I engage in cool reflection and do not simply do things on the spur of the moment but step back and say: 'What am I really doing? How could we do it still better?' In other words, I utilise the qualities of thinking ahead and reflection to a very great extent and build on reason.

The *integrated phase* demands that I interpret my perceptions and reflect on their meaning, that I analyse what lies behind them, that I stand outside myself and look over my shoulder critically or approvingly or listen to myself: 'What are you saying there? What are you actually doing here?'

Action in the integrated phase demands that we are conscious of ourselves, that we can reflect on what we are doing, on the sense or non-sense of our products and

41

services, on the sense or nonsense of requirements on which we have 'set our sights' simply to enrich ourselves. In other words, the ethics of our entrepreneurial action becomes a very important matter during the integrated phase, which comes to the fore with the *'consciousness soul'*. Rudolf Steiner describes how this cultural epoch began in Europe in the 15th century and will develop fully in the coming centuries. It brings with it growing ego-consciousness and the ability to overcome spiritual dependencies.

At the beginning of October 1992 I sent Bernard Lievegoed an outline of the fourth phase, the revised manuscript of his chapters and my additional work on the fourth phase. (He died on 12 December). We then had a brief correspondence on the question whether or not the development of an organisation to the 'consciousness soul' stage in our time could conceivably be followed by a further developmental phase. Hence he asked me: 'What do you see as the new consciousness stage?' For when we developed the integration concept we thought that this was the likely form for the present consciousness soul age in which people within organisations are challenged in their awareness, something which is reflected in a meaningful approach to the customer, the patient, the pupil or the market.

I answered Lievegoed that I had recently read a lecture by Rudolf Steiner which confirmed exactly what I had gradually developed as the concept of the fourth phase. Steiner describes how we are currently in the first stages of the challenges posed by the consciousness age, and that it is therefore necessary that in our social behaviour, in the structure of social organisations, we have to *look ahead to a later stage in the development of consciousness,* namely to the 'spirit-self culture'. He goes on to say how there is no other way, if we want to develop the present qualities to the full, than to anticipate and look ahead to future stages, because

Phases of the developing organisation

otherwise the attitude inherent in the consciousness soul can turn into a dreadfully egocentric stance.

Although we develop the desired qualities in our consciousness, it can easily happen that from a moral standpoint we fall back to earlier levels which we think we have already overcome. Thus we do not achieve the new ethical qualities to which we have access and which are demanded today. We have to overextend ourselves today, as it were, and even if we cannot yet do it we should already allow ourselves to the guided by those things which point beyond our consciousness soul culture.

In his lecture, Rudolf Steiner describes exactly the attitudes which are set out as the required new ethics in the book by Womack, Jones and Roos, *The Machine that changed the World*. I cannot only concentrate on the wellbeing of my own company but have to keep in mind the wellbeing of the associative network of enterprises. It has to be my concern to help the supplier along and also to assist the development of the customer. If they suffer, I suffer too – that is roughly what Womack, Jones and Roos say. Rudolf Steiner formulates it in the following way: In this new culture, this new consciousness, I will suffer down to a physical level when I know that people have been killed in Soweto, in Johannesburg or that people are dying in Sarajevo or starving in Calcutta. We will experience this in a very personal way. The only way we can manage the increase in our awareness in the age of the consciousness soul without becoming our neighbour's sworn enemy is to develop that faculty within ourselves. If my neighbour suffers I cannot simply carry on as if nothing had happened. His or her troubles will also be my concern in the age of the spirit-self.

I see another guiding principle in the associative phase: to bear real responsibility for the earth as an organism. It is no longer provocative to tell people that they should look beyond the end of their noses and over the garden fence of their own bourgeois world. After all, there are interesting descriptions of world models from an ecological perspective which state that we can only solve the major ecological problems if we look at the earth literally as a living organism as with the Gaia hypothesis (see J. Lovelock 1991). That is a further key thought in Rudolf Steiner's lecture mentioned above. In this way, by making brotherliness a part of our lives to an ever greater extent, we will gain access to a quite new encounter with Christ. It is precisely in economic matters, I would say, and in our political actions, precisely in those areas where we deal with the earth and its substance in a destructive or responsible and caring manner (not only in the celebration of a church service) that we work with the body of Christ. There we can meet or deny Christ. And where we handle natural resources with this awareness – this might sound a little poetic – that is where such work is really an act of transubstantiation. But to do this I need the awareness of the future 'spirit-self culture'.

The things I refer to here with such a new basic attitude as an anticipation of the spirit-self form of consciousness leads to the creation of new perceptual opportunities. What we can grasp with human intelligence can increasingly become an activity to develop senses which can grasp a cosmic, higher intelligence. In that way we can truly come closer to the spirit of our earth organism: Christ, who has connected Himself with us human beings and with our planet through the mystery of the crucifixion.

New problems call for new abilities!

At the beginning, I set out how the challenges of our time which have arisen with the collapse of the systems in neighbouring countries to the East are not over by a long way. These problems will still occupy us for decades. We should have no illusions about what it really means to live in this time of disruption, of losing the firm ground from under one's feet and of collapsing structures. That is so because it is clear that culturally too there must be radical change and transformation. In my view the debate about 'lean enterprises' has allowed new guiding principles and values to surface which should shake us up in our inner attitudes. For new organisational and cooperative forms in business also lead to a change of values, to cultural change.

I cannot undertake renewal if I do not have a different image of the human being and a different understanding of nature. Thus I have to question and abandon my present basic assumptions and well-worn patterns of thinking. I have to forget, discard, give up things and that always entails a stage of insecurity. I drift along and have lost the ground from under my feet.

That is why I said that it was important to have *inner* support, like with the trial by fire and air. In my view, one of these inner supports is a spiritual understanding of evolution. We are dealing with a more profound developmental understanding not only in the plant and animal realm, but above all in the human realm, in the social realm. I consider it to be very important that modern enterprises should have a picture of what is needed regarding cooperation, management and encounter with customers. Even if I cannot say which product will sell successfully in five or ten years from now, the way in which we manufacture, and the ways in which we develop ourselves, are very important. For then the work team will find the right answer, will develop the capacity to find answers even if I cannot yet give the answer today. The demands of this type of organisational development really imply that I – whether I am a manager or an employee representative, a politician or a member of staff – am active within the organisation which is going through that process. I have to understand that it is also up to me whether I participate actively in promoting change or whether I am dragged along in a course of events which I perhaps do not want in that form. Organisational development is a key area in structuring every type of organisation, in creating the ability to tackle and successfully manage future questions.

If we can manage to work in the way I have described, then there is less to worry about. When I see how the collapse of secure structures and values has provoked the very natural reactions of fear, anger, feelings of impotence, which are then worked off in violence, then this is not encouraging. I see a direct correlation between the increase in vandalism and racism and the collapse of traditional ideas and values. Much depends on whether this evolution can be conceived and implemented in work teams, in the economy and in the cultural sphere, so that people see themselves as responsible participants in the development towards an associative economy.

What I have described with the integrated and associative phases is precisely the opposite of totalitarianism. These phases represent an opportunity to realise social structures for free human beings. For in this period of structural change a massive battle is underway for the image we have of the human being.

New problems call for new abilities!

But it is in practice and not on theoretical proclamations that the basis for freedom or lack of it, for individual responsibility or totalitarian regulation, will be laid in the coming times. If I can find ways and means to play a responsible part in the conduct of my enterprise then I can increasingly build up, develop, anchor and consolidate this quality of self-determination and personal responsibility in at least this small community.

For the battle is already raging between heteronomy, determinism, the so-called force of circumstance on the one hand and and of self-determination on the other. If we do not remain vigilant in the European Union we face the threat of economic totalitarianism through over-commercialisation, including in the cultural sphere, which leads to an increase in outside control, in determinism to the degree of making human beings and society increasingly machine-like. A dangerous trend towards economic and political totalitarianism exists.

The other equally disastrous seduction is of course escapist egoism. It implies an unwillingness to be part of the community, to be part of the relationship of exchange and responsibility between the individual and the community. It says, 'Let me drop out, here is a piece of land where I can graze my lambs.' For to drop out represents a reaction of helplessness to the challenges of our time. It represents an ego trip in many forms, independence without commitment. Whether it is called one thing or another and couched in a variety of philosophical formulations is neither here nor there. The battle for the human image in real life takes place between these two polarised positions.

In reality, the crucial question separating the two is: 'Is there progress towards self-determination, self-actualisation, personal development, self-organisation, personal responsibility or are we on an ego trip away from

47

Enterprise of the future

Struggle for the human image in life

Egoism	Self-determination	Heteronomy
Independence, pleasure... lack of commitment	Freedom (self-actualisation, personal development...) with social responsibility	'Force of circumstance', 'economic laws compel...' determinism
...to the degree of dropping out of society	Individual human beings and society	...to the degree of making human beings and society increasingly machine-like
...ego trips	Community building on the basis of the power of the autonomous developing individual	...totalitarian systems

Figure 6: Struggle for the human image in life

New problems call for new abilities!

the requirements of our time?' There are no simple solutions to the dilemma of heteronomy and escapist egoism. All of us have to take a personal decision and after we have taken that decision we have to live daily with the reality of the answer we have found.

PART II

Moral intuition in organisational development and leadership

The contemporary relevance of the *Philosophy of Freedom: Intuitive Thinking as a Spiritual Path*

In reading, re-reading and reflecting on Rudolf Steiner's book *The Philosophy of Freedom*, I have realised with surprise that, far from being outdated 100 years later, this work has in fact gained in contemporary relevance. Our time is moved by the same questions of knowledge and ethics which occupied the end of the last century. The difference today is that the results of people's actions are much more dangerously far-reaching. What scientific research can do today could change the world dramatically in the sense that the irresponsible use of the knowledge gained in nuclear physics, for instance, or in genetic research could cause tremendous damage to human beings and nature. That was not the case to the same extent 100 years ago because the destructive nature of technological innovation was still locally restricted. A catastrophe on the scale of Chernobyl, in contrast, immediately becomes of global concern.

We are thus faced with the question: What are the issues which concern people today? What does contemporary thinking have to say about human knowledge and social action? What is considered to be the basis for ethical action in the dominant scientific currents of our time?

These hotly debated questions alone show that Steiner's work has not turned into an anachronism but touches on many contemporary topics. And what should, of course, cause us to stop and think is the fact that this book was

Enterprise of the future

written in its time for the future, as Steiner kept emphasising when the second edition appeared after the first world war. He wanted to give people something which would help them to face the challenges of the future. The work should thus be of significance for us today.

Now I cannot trawl too deeply in my remarks here, since my main concern is to illustrate how the *Philosophy of Freedom* illuminates the development and management of work communities, in other words, enterprises, local authorities, schools, churches and voluntary organisations. For that is the field of my professional activity as researcher, university teacher and management consultant, about which I can speak from experience.

To begin with, I will discuss the epistemological side of the *Philosophy of Freedom,* as Rudolf Steiner found it necessary to do in this work to create the basis for his ethical reflections. When I started reading the book, I often had difficulty with the way in which many of the formulations were tied to his time, but on re-reading it I found that, despite the outdated colouring of Steiner's language, things are expressed in a very succinct manner and are of great relevance in the contemporary struggle with epistemological questions. The second half of my discussion deals with the questions of freedom, morality and responsibility.

Belief in progress in 1894 and 1994

The western belief in progress before 1900 gave rise to the idea among many leading individuals that moral norms should be framed and made universally binding. Steiner stated, in contrast, that this could lead to the wrong solution for a problem which had been correctly diagnosed, because compulsory regulation should not be equated with moral development.

What, then, is the contemporary state of our belief in progress? Despite the post-modern growth in scepticism and concern, there continues to be a strong, almost superstitious belief in progress, even though the consequences of one-sided technological progress are already beginning to burden us in the form of ecological problems.

Let me quote some dramatic examples from contemporary thinkers. On the one hand we have the neurobiologists Humberto Maturana and Francisco Varela (1987), famous as representatives of 'epistemological radical constructivism'. Their theories have become the ruling fashion in the social sciences. Other well-known representatives of this current are the systems theorists H. von Foerster, N. Luhmann and H. Stierlin. Their epistemological understanding is diametrically opposed to that of the *Philosophy of Freedom* and calls, of course, for a serious response.

On the other hand there is the author and consultant Gerd Gerken from Worpswerde, well-known in Germany, who promotes a belief in progress on the basis of these ideas, which he calls 'kinetic management'. This seems highly dubious to me. He justifies this with his interpretation of 'cosmic evolution' (Gerken, 4-5/1991, p.1): 'Kinetic management translates the cosmic purpose of evolution into those realities which we invented previously.' And a little further on: 'Thus kinetic management is tied to the evolution of the spirit. In contrast, the ordinary type of management which predominates today is not tied to the evolution of the spirit. Kinetic management, however, uses precisely the spirit as its primary instrument because it is *management by invention*.'

Gerken polemicises against the environmental movement and criticises it as 'Bambi-ecology' which he contrasts with his so-called 'critical ecology' (Gerken, 4-5/1991, p.5): 'Critical environmentalists criticise classical green ecology as a backward looking environmental movement driven by feelings of guilt, a one-sided repair-ecology based on a rather sentimental transfiguration of nature... "Bambi" ecology... Critical ecologists have a different understanding of nature. (...) They do not want self-accusation, denial of progress. They do not want "low tech" or "no tech" but the progressive transformation of our technology, in other words, more high tech, bio-technology and genetic engineering.' Then on page 6: 'The critical ecologists together with those engaged in genetic research have discovered the secret of the "cosmic purpose". This new concept says that nature basically always shows dissipating dynamics.' This leads Gerd Gerken to the conclusion (p. 7):

'1. We are allowed to destroy.
2. We should do it more intelligently than we have done so far.

From this perspective there is, in principle, neither a global environmental crisis nor the drama of the world ending...'

I will return later to Gerken's other arguments and conclusions. But it is easy to understand that such words give welcome ammunition to company managements, faced with the accusation that they are contributing to the destruction of the biosphere, to argue for the continuation of their environmentally destructive actions. I have quoted Maturana, Varela and Gerken here because they are symptomatic of a way of thinking, and action based on such thinking. Such thinking sets the tone today and can be uncritically accepted by many of our contemporaries. The usefulness of Steiner's *Philosophy of Freedom* becomes evident in debate with the latter. The confusing thing is that many thinkers of our time – such as Gerken, Maturana and Varela and New-Age authors – use a vocabulary which at first sight appears identical with Steiner's concepts. They speak of 'spirit', 'spirituality', 'evolution', 'cosmic intelligence', 'intuition', 'thinking', etc.; only closer inspection reveals that they mean something completely different from Steiner.

When Maturana and Varela speak of 'spirit' they are referring to the cultural product which is the joint creation of organisms with the gift of language (Maturana, Varela 1987, p.250) and not to a reality which exists independently of human beings. When Gerken writes about 'spirituality' he is referring to human intelligence as the 'highly complex dynamic interplay of many currents' which is to be enhanced through 'evolution' (Gerken 4-5/1991, p.7). And the concept of 'intuition', much used by many modern therapeutic streams, is as a rule understood as the irrational and emotional element of the human psyche in contrast to the rational side. Human 'thinking' is deprived in principle of the ability to know truth because according to the theses of epistemological constructivism, which bases itself on the findings of neurophysiology, we are dealing merely with subjective constructs which, according to Bernd Schmid (Schmid 1989, p.50), '...are produced through the thinking, experience and action of the people concerned'. Schmid continues: 'Radical constructivism assumes, rather, that realities are always stabilised habits which help us to orientate ourselves and explain social systems whose purpose is to organise life and survival but which have nothing to do with any objective reality.' (Schmid 1989, p.51).

These concepts illustrate the current state of the scientific debate and the means by which it defines its own scientific basis.

The contemporary relevance of epistemology

I will deal, to begin with, with the basic concepts of the *Philosophy of Freedom:* perception, intuition, thinking. How does Steiner define them and what is their epistemological relevance? As a searching, inquiring person I perceive certain objects with my physical senses on the one hand; on the other hand I combine those individual percepts through my thinking with another reality, with the world of ideas. That represents one of the core theses of the *Philosophy of Freedom* (p. 73):
'The separate facts appear in their true significance, both in themselves and for the rest of the world, only when thinking spins its threads from one entity to another (...) In contrast to the content of the percept which is given to us from without, the content of thinking appears inwardly. The form in which this first makes its appearance we will call intuition.'
What we perceive both on a sensory and psychological level is 'dismembered' as it were by our sensory perception and distorted because our eyes, ears and sense of touch, can only take in certain parts or sections of comprehensive reality because of the way that human beings are physically organised. Perception has to be one-sidedly reductionist and distorting because it can only ever grasp extracts of a whole. What we perceive can only be placed in a context and grasped as something whole, something meaningful, through the act of thinking (p. 74): 'To explain a thing, to make it intelligible, means nothing else than to place it into the context from which it has been torn by the peculiar character of our organisation as already described ...'

Only intuition and thinking can establish a connection in space and time and turn the process of sensory dismemberment back into a whole again (p. 100-101): 'The laws of nature are just such connections. (...) Through my perceiving (...) as subject, I am confronted with the object. The connection of things is thereby interrupted. The subject restores this connection by means of thinking.'

It is not denied, then, that objective knowledge is possible in principle through the interaction of perception and thinking. However, it is a life-long task to refine one's perceptual ability by embarking on a path of training and development such as is the purpose of Steiner's exercises or the eightfold path of the Buddha, among others. The reflective thinker, too, has to become aware of the likely and possible corruption of thinking activity through culturally determined habits of reflection, through wishful thinking, projection and introjection, rationalisation etc, and has to be purified. The properties which the constructivist approach to reality sees as a fundamental part of perception and thinking can, in the light of the *Philosophy of Freedom*, quite correctly be applied to the state of thinking and perception before the path of strict and systematic self-purification has been started. In situations of social conflict relations break down because each one of the parties to the conflict is convinced that its (subjectively coloured) view of things represents the truth as such and that the other party is consciously falsifying and distorting things (Glasl 1990). Constructivist theory thus perfectly describes pathological situations in which subjective perceptions determined by particular interests are not corrected through purified thinking which is committed to logic and truth. But I consider it to be scientifically inadmissible to declare pathological patterns of perception and thinking to be characteristic of human perception and thinking as such.

The contemporary relevance of epistemology

This kind of relationship between perception and thinking is, after all, something which preoccupies the whole of the scientific world, irrespective of whether we are dealing with questions concerning psycho-social therapies or management and organisation theory, whether we are dealing with nuclear physics or genetic research. The answers which are given by many scientists mostly lead to a form of epistemological neo-dualism ('The cognitive subject can never recognise the thing in itself but is divided from it by an unbridgeable gulf'), or to a neo-materialism which tries to explain all knowledge by means of neurophysiological conditions and sees no place for an act of the spirit.

One hundred years ago, the *Philosophy of Freedom* indicated the path to be followed. I quote from it on the fundamental questions concerning the relationship between object, subject, perception and thinking (p. 108): 'The reader will gather from what has gone before, but even more from what will follow, that "percept" is here taken to be everything that approaches man through the senses or through the spirit, before it has been grasped by the actively elaborated concept.'

The radical constructivism (Maturana, Varela 1987, p.258) described earlier reduces knowledge to something which is created through the structure '...of the nervous system operating as a closed system' which is 'produced' or 'co-defined' in communication with other human beings. Furthermore: *'Understanding the nature of knowledge places an obligation on us.* It places an obligation on us to maintain constant vigilance to avoid the temptation of certainty. It obliges us to admit that our certainties are no evidence of truth, that the world which everyone sees is not *the* world but *a* world which we produce together' (Maturana, Varela, p. 263-264).

According to this theory, anything described as spiritual is only a construct which we personally build. Steiner, in contrast, presents the understanding of the nature of knowledge in a different light (p. 122): 'Intuition is the conscious experience – in pure spirit – of a purely spiritual content. Only through intuition can the essence of thinking be grasped.'

Gestalt psychology often uses the following picture (Figure 7) as illustration of the facts which Steiner describes as the activity of intuition and thinking.

If we look at the picture without preconceptions, we see various dots, lines with spaces in between, triangles, etc. on a white surface. Only when we ask the question whether these dots and lines might be signs of something else do we recognise a number in the multiplicity of forms even if it can not be pinned down precisely. Something extra happens in us. When we look at the picture we, as cognitive subjects, connect these dots and lines into something which becomes meaningful, however unclear the sensory perception. This happens because we activate our thinking in addition to our sensory perception. The linking together of sensory perceptible signs, which we experience in the first instance as disconnected, is only possible through the action of intuition and thinking. As a consequence it would not even be possible for Maturana and Varela to develop their theory of constructivism if it really were impossible for the thinking to become active in the sense formulated by Steiner. That is also demonstrated by their appeal to 'logical bookkeeping' (Maturana, Varela, p.148), that is, their appeal to a logic which logically cannot itself be the product of these constructs. Maturana and Varela do not manage without reference to ideas either, such as the idea of organisations, of structure, autopoiesis or the self-generation of living beings. (Maturana, Varela 1987, p. 49ff.)

The contemporary relevance of epistemology

Gestalt Figure

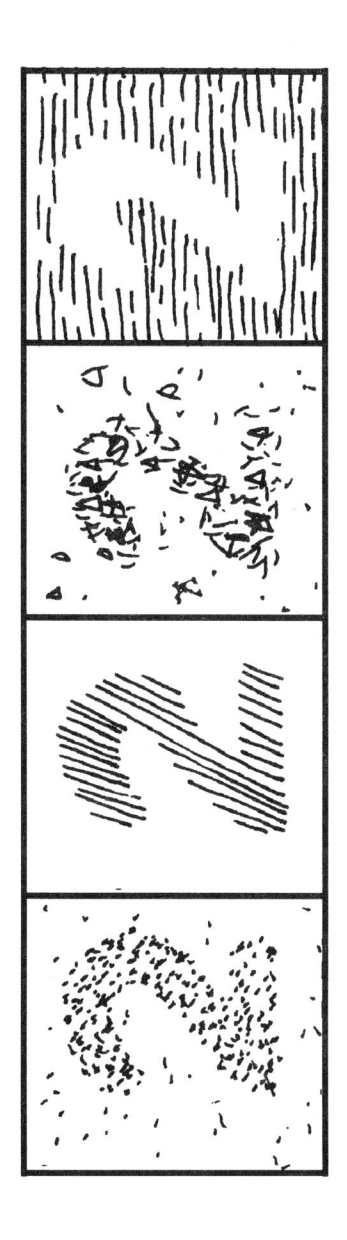

Figure 7: Gestalt Figure

Enterprise of the future

What we take in, according to Steiner, as a series of individual details divided through the manifold nature of our perceptions, is joined together again through thinking. For it lies in the nature of thinking that it can enter the reality of the spirit also without the mediation of the sensory apparatus of perception. Thinking as a spiritual act is actually the communion of the spiritual element in human beings with the spiritual element in the world because they are the same by nature. That is why thinking can build a bridge at all between the spiritual element in the world and the spiritual element in human beings. After all, as subject I participate in the same spiritual reality as the object. That is the monism which Rudolf Steiner later refers to when he attempts to characterise his approach. Steiner's original text (p. 73), which I have already quoted above, puts it like this: 'The separate facts appear in their true significance, both in themselves and for the rest of the world, only when thinking spins its threads from one entity to another.'

That is what we did in looking at Figure 7 when we recognised the number 'two' behind the dots and lines. Thinking thus means nothing less than making whole again a perceived object which has of necessity been broken up in the cognitive subject by our sensory perception. Here it can be instructive to look at the origin of the word 'whole'. 'Whole', in middle and old high German is *heil*, in Dutch *heel* means 'intact, healthy'. Thinking is a holistic, that is, a healing activity – in contrast to the popular description of thinking in *Gestalt therapy* for instance as 'invention', 'fantasising' and suchlike.

Rudolf Steiner shows what else happens through the spiritual action of thinking (p. 100-101): 'The laws of nature are just such connections. (...) Through my perceiving (...) as subject, I am confronted with the object. The connection of things is thereby interrupted. The subject restores this connection by means of thinking.'

Practical application of epistemology

Thinking creates this communion between the spiritual element in human beings and the spiritual element in the world and thereby enables the discovery of the laws of nature even if they keep having to be re-formulated through subsequent research findings. For knowledge is – as Karl Popper (1957/II, p.272ff.) also says – an *evolutionary process of discovering the truth*. We have to keep doubting and questioning current findings and subjecting them to public debate in order to approach truth in larger or smaller steps even if we can never grasp it outright: 'But that does not mean that *truth* is "relative". It only means that most scientific results have the character of hypotheses, in other words, of propositions whose proof is insufficient and which are therefore open to revision at any time.' (Popper 1957).

Practical application of epistemology in organisational consultancy work

The practical benefit of Steiner's understanding of perception and thinking can be experienced in consultancy work. In the early seventies, I and my colleague at that time, Dirk Lemson, developed a self-diagnosis method, the so-called 'U-procedure' (Figure 8), at the NPI-Institute for Organisational Development. This procedure enables people actively to question and improve their work in their organisations.

To begin with, we have to choose a quite concrete and clearly comprehensible work process which we then examine with the U-procedure. With the first step we investigate the given situation, i.e. the physical reality of the *technical and instrumental sub-system* of an organisation (processes, tools, material resources and plant); with the second step we look at the way in which the *social sub-system* is constituted (individual functions and organs, the character of individuals, of management and relationships, the social architecture of the fledgling organisation); with the third step we create an explicit awareness of the *cultural sub-system,* in other words, the basic assumptions, values and attitudes which have hitherto been implicitly lived in the organisation.

With **Question 1** concerning the technical and instrumental sub-system we can, for instance, examine the concrete process of how the authors of a certain book came together, how they debated among themselves, when the idea

Organisational development:
'The spirit in matter becomes visible, the new idea works within matter!'

Self-diagnosis and planning through the 'U-procedure'

(Glasl / Lemson)

What is		**What we want**
1. How do processes and work flows function? Instruments, resources	**Technical and instrumental sub-system**	7. How can processes be developed in future?
⇩		⇧
2. ...and how are functions, roles and management distributed?	**Social sub-system**	6. ...what does that mean for new functions and roles?
⇩		⇧
3. According to which implicit/actual values, rules does this happen?	**Cultural sub-system**	5. What values and guidelines do we want for the future?
⇘		⇗
	4. Is this what we want?	

Figure 8: The U-Procedure

Practical application of epistemology

of publication came up and the first discussion with the publisher took place, how the chapters were then worked up, proofs read etc. The work process and the way it was supported by PCs, fax machines, telephones, paper flow and many other things is very seriously reconstructed. In a larger organisation this work will take place in several parallel groups which later exchange and debate their results. It is exceedingly important that this reconstruction should be undertaken with great precision.

With *Question 2,* we examine the same process but now from the perspective of who took on which tasks, who had what possibilities to exercise influence and make decisions and what roles were played in relation to one another. What roles were created consciously or unconsciously, were they wanted or not? How did they fit together? How did the authors and the supporting staff treat one another as people? The social sub-system can be described using this method.

Question 3 takes the descriptions of 1 and 2 and deepens them: we watch ourselves like an inquisitive and critical journalist from a secret hiding place and try to grasp the unwritten rules and principles according to which everything is organised. Here we come to the unspoken assumptions, guidelines, values and policies for action of everyone concerned. These can be individually formulated as mottos or rules, as imperatives for thinking and action. For example: 'As long as people fantasise about a beautiful book without commitment to action everyone is motivated and involved – as soon as commitment is required and work needs to be done everyone disappears into thin air.' Or: 'If there is work to be distributed, wait until last with your suggestion, for the person who speaks first is always lumbered with it.'

Those could be some of the practical norms or guidelines which inform a person's action. If we are honest, we formulate many rules for action which do not always sound

Enterprise of the future

pleasant or which stand in contradiction to declared principles ('We bear all burdens jointly'). A key element in working with the U-procedure is that we should be honest with ourselves and do not embellish the real situation or falsify it in self-justification.

Question 4 demands a binding answer from every person which takes part in this conversation: Do we want things to continue as before? Do we stand by our fundamental philosophy or do we want to change it? Are we prepared to take personal responsibility if the basic principles do not change? The norms and values which have been written down are individually looked at and examined in order to decide which ones should remain, which ones should perhaps be strengthened and which ones should be replaced by new ones.

The previous steps of Questions 1 and 2 have led us to the hidden spiritual basis of social reality, to the real thinking, feeling and will of a community. Even if quite different work processes are handled separately by different groups which then present their results, including Question 4, to one another, the same puzzling phenomenon occurs: on the level of Question 3 they produce completely consistent principles as the basis of their daily practice. For this reason I prefer to investigate processes which belong to the routine actions of the day, in a hospital for instance the daily washing of bed-ridden patients, the serving of meals, the doctors' visit. When the consistency of the values which underlie the actions of the people concerned is uncovered, it always produces great surprise: How can this be explained?

We are working at three levels of reality: physical reality, psycho-social reality, spiritual reality. There is thus a spiritual reality behind the diverse reality which is accessible to the senses, a spiritual reality which allows us to see how everything is connected. It is like a network of groundwater

Practical application of epistemology

which creates subterranean connections between otherwise diverse landscapes. If I dig through the two upper layers, I will always arrive at the same 'groundwater zone' which is the spiritual foundation of an organisation. When they exchange their partial results, people notice that their statements tend to sound similar. It is almost as if they were speaking in chorus. The U-procedure allows us to gain access to this third reality and to enter a dialogue about it.

As we proceed, we then elaborate in accordance with *Question 5* of the U-procedure how the rules or values which people want for the future should sound. We do not therefore proceed straight away to the transformation of concrete processes (Question 7), but reflect on the fundamental changes which should take place (Question 5) and their consequences for functions and roles which have to be newly defined (Question 6). Only then do we move to concrete processes which have to be newly designed.

As a result, people experience that it is not chance which determines what comes out at the end, but the attitude of truthfulness of all those engaged in the investigation. As long as individual people twist, hide or deny certain behaviours because they want them 'construed' in a certain way, they will feel a certain resistance in the group. The group's attitude can be defined as the practice of 'evolutionary insight'. This spiritual experience then is not something abstract or academic for those involved, but they are able to experience in a practical way how their perception has lead to clarification through intuition and thinking.

The hubris of constructivism

The fathers of constructivism often emphasise that their philosophy is against every kind of fundamentalism and totalitarianism. They say that, on the contrary, it forms the basis of a universal attitude of tolerance as is required in democratic societies. For this philosophy assumes that we simply cannot gain any knowledge of truth:

1. Because the nervous system does not interact in any way with the external world of objects since it operates as a closed system in every biological organism

2. Because on the basis of the way that the nervous system functions we must never assume that our ideas can reflect (represent) anything of the objects which we perceive with our senses; for the electro-chemical processes within the nervous system can never ever transport an object into our brain and our life of ideas

3. Because as a consequence all perceptions, feelings, ideas and thoughts are in the first instance products of our inner life, that is, constructs which we as living beings use to preserve ourselves in, and adapt ourselves to, our environment

4. Because all concepts which we form are only created through language in a process of joint 'linguification' of social systems; thus concepts are also constructs of our sensory and nervous processes and conventions; what we have not recognised for ourselves does not represent reality to us; without the cognitive person there is no reality.

The evidence for this case comes from biology, or to be more precise, from neurophysiology. In brief, the argument (in essence according to Maturana, Varela 1987, p.145ff., Maturana 1988) against any possibility of our sensory and thought impressions being true states: 'Don't have any illusions! What you perceive has nothing whatsoever to do with the object outside your body. The nervous system is not a dispatch system by which information or objects can be transported to the brain. From the first sensory impressions which your sensors gain of a thing the pressure, heat, light, sound, etc. is transformed into chemical or electrical processes which occur in and between the neurons in your organism. What finally becomes ideas and concepts in your brain via these neurological pathways simply cannot have the slightest connection with the object which your senses perceived. And if as a consequence you undertake some sort of action this again results in constant transformations in your nervous system until a muscle moves. Thus what comes to expression in your behaviour cannot have any identity either with the object which you originally perceived.'

I like to contrast this with the following simple comparison: I have spoken with my wife on the telephone and we have told one another that after 28 years of marriage we still stand by our 'yes' because quite different dimensions of love and partnership have become visible in our relationship than were evident at the time of our engagement. When the radical constructivist sees me smiling happily at the end of that telephone conversation he says: 'You think that your wife loves you? Don't kid yourself! For what came out at your end of the telephone has nothing whatsoever to do with what was spoken into the receiver at the other end. Just think for a moment of the way the microphone works, the electro-magnets, the electrical current, the telephone wire, then the amplification through transistors, through to

The hubris of constructivism

the diaphragm of your telephone receiver. That cannot be the same thing!'

I can answer that by saying: My wife's intended message, her simple declaration of love, arrived at my end no matter whether it came by telephone, television, smoke signals or in a bottle. Because the acoustic or visual signals are carriers of words and ideas, her thoughts and intentions can reach me as she broadly intended, irrespective of the particular technical nature of the means of transmission. That does not require a biochemical transmission to take place via the telephone line in order to enable a quasi physical encounter. Since our acoustic signals signify words and these words concepts, we can enter into these concepts during the telephone conversation regardless of the frailty of the transmission technology.

That is also how I envisage the interconnection of physical and sensory perception which is tied to the body and the spiritual activity of thinking. Without the spiritual acts of thinking as described by Steiner we would all be imprisoned solipsistically in our bodies in lifelong solitary confinement.

The final consequence of the constructivist view of perception and thinking is that scientific research becomes meaningless. If there is no approach to truth but at most a relativistic exchange of views we might as well remove the research budget from all state finances. That, at one blow, would help to save enormous sums of money.

We can see the results which the final consequences of such a philosophy would have on the spiritual life of society: The reality of spiritual matters has no objective content, so it can be manipulated at will. In contrast, Steiner's thesis that thinking enables one to begin to approach truth leads to the conclusion that the search for truth must not be restricted, pre-determined or censored by political or economic interests because otherwise cultural and spiritual life cannot fulfil its innovative core functions in society. It would become the submissive servant of politics and business. To put it in exaggerated terms, constructivism leads to the conclusion that no world exists outside my world of ideas, just as small children often believe that it gets dark in the world when they close their eyes. In classical philosophy this view is described as 'solipsism' because it is based on the premise that 'only I exist'. And although the fathers of constructivism often emphasise that their theory does not lead to solipsism, it does undoubtedly do so. The constructivists always point out that other people besides me exist with their experiences and concepts which logically would have to be compatible – nevertheless, they do not succeed in making the credible claim within their conceptual system that a world is able to exist in front of me, next to me and behind me even if I myself do not exist as a perceiving subject.

At first sight, then, constructivism appears to be democratically tolerant because it rejects any kind of claim to absolute truth and only admits to relative truths. But Karl Popper (1957) very accurately points out that this – in contrast to the stated intention – is the first step to totalitarian behaviour. Because if there is no point in testing the proximity to truth of a statement through a process of public investigation and debate, only one decisive factor remains in society: one has to have the power to enforce one's own view. The attempt at legitimisation and refutation is fundamentally a senseless undertaking. Such relativistic tolerance promotes naked violence. In addition, I can unscrupulously place all scientific activity in the service of political or economic interests and can define the laws of nature as best accords with my own interests. If I can ensure that the 'laws of nature' which I have defined in this way are generally accepted in society then they are correct. Here the modesty of relativism is revealed as hubris.

The hubris of constructivism

In this context I quote once again Gerd Gerken, the consultant to whom we have already referred (4-5/1991, p.2): 'We thought, for example, for a long time that the so-called laws of nature are somehow anchored in nature, that nature is organised mathematically for reasons which remain a mystery. Now we are beginning to realise that this mathematical order is projected into nature by ourselves, that we have not discovered it but, at best, rediscovered it.' We can see that this is a logical conclusion from a constructivist point of view. In this sense the sciences have actually played a nasty trick on us: they put the rabbit of the laws of nature which they made themselves into nature, in order then – naughty! naughty! – to pull it out again as the discovery of a law. Gerken continues, following Vilém Flusser: 'If we discover that the law of free fall obeys a geometrical progression, because this is a category of our thinking, we can just as well set ourselves the task of finding another solution.' Here we witness the leap from relativistic modesty to the idea of human omnipotence. Gerken further writes: 'After all, nowhere does it say that the laws of nature have to be exactly as we have already formulated them. We can make other laws of nature. We can dredge up alternative orders. I can make what orders I want. And I can make them as convenient as possible. Copernicus is not more true than Ptolemy, simply more convenient. Thus Vilém Flusser.' And finally (p. 16): 'We can see, therefore, that the evolution of the spirit (for example in the form of improving our ethics) is directly connected with the ability of our managers to improve the world ... to improve it through future-oriented management ... to improve it through mega courage.'

Gerken's own expression, 'mega courage', in fact unmasks his theses as hubris, as boundless self over-estimation and presumption. The laws of nature have been left completely at the mercy of human feasibility. And because Gerken sees it in this way he fights Christian ethics as a body of knowledge which paralyses through guilt feelings, and he propagates 'new ethical values of free spirituality' (p.14) because the economic system cannot be controlled by ethics but only by itself.: 'The morality of the market is precisely that it has no morality' (p. 17).

In my work with managers and their staff I like to undertake an exercise in the observation of nature. Together with Jürgen Dillmann, who as a teacher of horticulture at the Salzburg Waldorf School is a sound specialist in botany, we ask people to study individual plant leaves – of the poppy for instance – and to order them according to their own criteria. (Bockemühl 1973) In ordering the leaves, the people always arrive at the conclusion that certain leaves somehow belong together and form groups, but that then certain gaps exist which leave questions open regarding classification. And it is precisely at this point that they discover that their thinking can grasp patterns and characteristics which provide effective developmental principles in nature. The liberating and beneficial element in this and similar exercises is that people discover that their perception gives them access to elements which together with their thinking give them an insight into natural relationships which are neither constructs nor the arbitrary products of their imaginations. On the contrary, it leads to the firm ground of spiritual facts and not to airy-fairy fantasies. This experience gives people a feeling of trust: the world is not accidental, arbitrary and chaotic. The laws of biology are, in principle, no different to those of astronomy, music or the developmental phases of the human being. The world is interconnected and I as human being am included in that. We enter a world by means of the thinking which can have universal validity if we succeed in overcoming our wishes and interests, our habits and conveniences. This exercise allows us to experience the necessary polarity of

The hubris of constructivism

body and spirit, of perception and thinking, of part and context. And we can experience that these polarities are not polarised divisions, but that they can be combined fruitfully through the soul activity of human beings. For perception and thinking have to be activated by the human will which is guided by the 'I'. The 'I' as spiritual core of the human being can communicate, i.e. be in communion, with the spiritual element in the rest of the world via thinking.

In modern computer technology, 'cyberspace' is attracting a lot of attention. A special visor makes it possible for us to see a three-dimensional space. As soon as we move our head to the left this movement is transferred to the computer through sensors which then produces a picture as if we were looking towards the left side of the space. If we take a few steps the computer transfers this movement into a change in the picture to give the impression as if we were entering the space. If we move our arms, we can create the illusion of flying through that space etc. Flight simulators for pilot training are such cyberspace machines.

If I now assume the standpoint of radical constructivism, it is no longer possible to distinguish why such simulation of 'virtual space' should be any less real than any other image which my fantasy projects on to the screen of my imagination. Whether I imagine a glass of water or whether it really stands before me is one and the same thing. There is no difference between perception and illusion. If I cannot solve certain problems, if the world has been environmentally destroyed, we can take the most beautiful holidays in natural landscapes which have been conjured up in cyberspace. It is therefore logical for Gerd Gerken to welcome the development of cyberspace as a cultural drug.

The ego-less individual

It is the aim of the *Philosophy of Freedom* to create the basis for the maximum degree of individual freedom and responsibility. This is because, given the appropriate development, the 'I' as the spiritual core of every human being provides access to knowledge which is the precondition for moral action.

The constructivists reject the concept of an 'I' which has existential qualities of its own. That is why Maturana and Varela say, when they attempt to explain the appearance of a 'self' in the development of human beings and humankind (Maturana, Varela 1987, p.240ff.): 'Thus in the intimacy of recursive individual interaction which personalises the other individual through a linguistic distinction like a name, the conditions may have been present for the appearance of a self as a distinct entity in the linguistic field.' And later (p. 249) they conclude, '...that there is no self-consciousness without language as a phenomenon of linguistic recursion. Self-consciousness, consciousness, spirit – those are phenomena which take place in language. That is why they only occur as such in the social sphere (...) That shows us in a dramatic way that it is in language that a self, an "I" is created (...) as socially unique ...'

Deciphered, that means: the 'I' does not exist as such, it is a product of language and this is to be equated with spirit. Varela expressed it in much more extreme terms in an interview in Vienna in June 1994 (Varela 1994): 'There you go through your whole life and think that you possess an "I" – but on a physiological and molecular level there is no trace of it. The deeper one penetrates into the brain the less one finds a subject, a central point at which everything converges...' And on the basis of the constructivist view of perception, of the way that from a neurophysiological perspective sensory perceptions are constructed in the multiplicity of the neurons, he compares ego-less perception and thinking with a jazz band: 'One can imagine it like a jazz band, like an ensemble which plays together without a conductor when suddenly new tones come from the outside which are integrated into the context of the music and are structured by it.'

The comparison with the jazz band as illustration of the lack of an 'I' shows very clearly where the cardinal failure of constructivism lies. For if I take the jazz band with the logic of Varela the neurophysiologist and take the instruments to pieces I cannot find the tune anywhere which is taken up and modulated by the musicians. Worse still, when I take the clarinet and trumpet and piano apart I find lots of physical and mechanical pieces but nowhere a single note! If seek an understanding of the music by taking the instruments apart I can find no tones, no music whatsoever. The tones are created only when a musician with a certain intention makes the reed vibrate by blowing across it. And the apparently conductorless harmony of the jazz musicians can certainly not be understood if we ignore that their playing was preceded by agreement on a key, a subject and numerous other compositional rules. What the subject represents as spiritual reality for the music and the use of the musical instruments, the 'I' represents as spiritual reality for the use of the nervous system and other bodily functions for the thinking. The music cannot be explained on the basis of the physical instruments but the activity of the instruments is explained by what is intended with the music, just as the thinking does not produce the spirit but the spirit produces the thinking and in doing so makes use of the neurophysiological instruments. Therefore it is ludicrous to seek the 'I' in the physical cells and molecules.

The ego-less individual

This example shows that constructivism as materialist philosophy is trapped by its own premises. Nevertheless, Maturana and Varela argue at the end of their fundamental book for an ethic of love as the consequence of their epistemological approach, because love underlies everything in the social sphere. Without love we would not tolerate or seek one another in the social sphere, without love we would not exchange our thoughts through language. And it pleases me that at this point I can agree for once with one of Maturana's and Varela's ideas!

Moral intuition

Our paths diverge again, however, when we look at the moral basis of human actions. The conclusions which Gerken draws concerning action from his perspective have already been indicated in several places in my earlier explanations. We saw that in his view it is necessary to realise what he calls the 'cosmic purpose of evolution', namely to enhance human intelligence at any cost: the ethics of the future are to have no ethics. Following Niklas Luhmann, Gerken writes (4-5/1991, p.19): '...That there is, rightly, growing doubt about the justification of ethics and morality. It was increasingly uncertain today "whether the distinction between good and bad is in turn good or bad"... As Luhmann says, it is precisely the task of this "new ethics to limit the sphere of morality; indeed, its most pressing task is to warn of morality."'

Constructivism as it has been quoted here sees the source of social action in the individual's or a community's interest to conform and live their life, and he recommends mutual communication, negotiation and coordination while supposed certainties are continuously called into question. Yet in the last instance it is paradoxically violence – as Karl Popper has shown – which remains the means to impose one's will on other people.

If a theory is based on the view that all knowledge is determined by the physical organism, then the impulses for action can only come from that physical side. That is, indeed, confirmed to a certain degree by our everyday experience. When I have eaten a cheese fondue I feel differently and am inclined to act differently than when I have eaten something light. A physically based driving force is considered to be the determining factor behind our actions.

Rudolf Steiner once again starts with the polarity of the human being's physical organisation and his/her spiritual being. There are physical triggers for action which are countered from the spiritual side with ideas and motives for action (p. 124): 'In any particular act of will we must take into account the motive and the driving force. The motive is a factor with the character of a concept or a mental picture; the driving force is the will-factor belonging to the human organisation and directly conditioned by it.'

Our actions can, of course, be determined solely by our physical drives. Then we act unconsciously or semi-consciously, instinctively and dominated by our physical urges. But it is also possible that by training the spiritual and soul part of ourselves we become increasingly guided in our actions by ideas and concepts. Where the latter is the case the motives of moral conduct are mental images and concepts (p. 128/129): 'But if we act under the influence of intuitions, the driving force of our action is pure thinking... For what is here effective as the driving force is no longer something merely individual in me, but the ideational and hence universal content of my intuition... The motives of moral conduct are mental pictures and concepts.'

The concept of moral intuition is very important for my work with people and their organisations. That can be demonstrated by means of my practical working methods.

I place particular value on working out a vision of the future by letting people think about the following questions individually and in groups:

> What would you like to have achieved within the next three years?
> What do you dream of?
> What do you really want to live for – personally as well as regarding your function in the company?

Moral intuition

These questions can encourage people to imagine certain pictures and to make a note of them. They contain – initially in an embryonic and vague form – their moral intuitions which will later receive a firmer outline. Then I create a great panorama from these dream-like ideals and future expectations to the past and ask: Looking back on the past seven years, what changes have you noticed in yourself and your environment? What trends have become evident? This question too is initially answered individually. Then it is exchanged in small groups which have built up a relationship of mutual trust and it is further deepened through discussion. Then every person looks back at their abilities in the most recent past: What did you succeed in? What went completely or almost wrong? What abilities do you take with you from the past into the future? What do you owe to your physical attributes?

The next question is devoted to the feedback and comments which come from the most important people in your environment who have a lively interest in ensuring your further development: What do these people wish from you? What are they asking you? What feedback are you getting from them?

Now the point is not that as a person totally under outside control you simply do what others want you to do. Rather, you should examine that question in order to clarify your own wishes in relation to it. For the next step in determining your objectives is to describe in concepts and images how the future which you seek to achieve will look two years hence if everything goes according to plan. That requires moral imagination. It is given even more concrete form by asking: What concrete steps will you take in the next few days, tomorrow?

This is followed in group discussion by the so-called 'shake-up': The members of the group raise all kinds of obstacles and excuses which could prevent the realisation of those aims. In other words, the members of the group allow the saboteur within themselves to speak. Moral equipment is now required in order to describe in clear and concrete terms what could be done to counter those obstacles. Thus mental images and concepts of the motivation which guides our actions are created in intensive group discussion.

The important thing here, as Rudolf Steiner emphasises, is that we are not guided by moral conventions which are ideologically bound for instance to the 'general good', 'progress', 'humanitarian values' and suchlike but that we first listen to the pure intuition which can be grasped by the spiritual core of our being (p. 132): 'The highest conceivable moral principle, however, is one that from the start contains no such reference (e.g: to general good, progress, etc.) but springs from the source of pure intuition and only later seeks any reference to percepts, to life.' Binding common principles, laws, objectives and norms can quite easily be agreed subsequently on the basis of these individual impulses (p. 134): 'The decisive factor of an intuitively determined action in any concrete instance is the discovery of the corresponding purely individual intuition. At this level of morality one can only speak of general concepts of morality (standards, laws) in so far as these result from the generalisation of the individual impulses.'

As human beings we therefore have to have the courage to go along an individual path of searching and questioning and not to follow given norms and simplistic slogans. As a result, what Steiner formulates as follows becomes possible (p. 132-133): 'The action is therefore neither a stereotyped one which merely follows certain rules, nor is it one which we automatically perform in response to an external impulse, but it is an action determined purely by its own ideal content.'

The potential for conflict in communities

It is clear that these words describe a state which can be achieved as the result of far-reaching individual and social development. Therefore it is used in my work as an objective, as the distant destination against which to measure my actions as a consultant. It means that a great deal is expected of the individual. In principle everyone has an equal possibility to find intuition. Thus Steiner also calls this vision 'ethical individualism'.

But a sense of reality also dictates that we examine the extent to which a community can already do justice to these demands. I know many communities which have set themselves such high moral objectives and therefore reject any kind of restriction of individual freedom through community regulation. The result is many types of conflict in these communities. Since one of the special areas of my consultancy work is to advise on how to overcome conflicts in organisations, I have examined the problem in detail. Conflict arises when several factors come together which I will describe briefly here:

1. People demand that their individual intuitions are respected but at the same time deny their colleagues a similar ability to come to intuitions according to their best efforts.

This becomes evident in schools for example, when an inner circle is formed which thinks of itself as further advanced than everyone else and has to protect itself against other people who are considered to be less mature in their soul and spiritual development. This attitude of self-satisfied 'moralising' contradicts Rudolf Steiner's thinking (p.138/139): 'What this kind of moralist does not understand is the unity of the world of ideas. He does not see that the world of ideas working in me is no other than the one working in my fellow human being. (...) I differ from my fellow human being not because we are living in two entirely different spiritual worlds but because from the world of ideas common to us both we receive different intuitions. He wants to live out his intuition, I mine. (...) Only the morally unfree who follow their natural instincts or the accepted demands of duty come into conflict with their neighbours if these do not obey the same instincts and the same commands as themselves.

2. People preach at one another while assuming dishonest motives and driving forces in the others.

This attitude is linked with the above moralising. One's own attitude is of course seen as clean and beyond reproach while the other person's attitude is perceived with disapproval. Basically the person who refers to his own moral intuitions attempts to impose a heteronomous norm of behaviour on the other person, namely what the former thinks is good for the latter. The community is split by such contradictions and paradoxes. It provides the breeding ground for 'carrying out hot conflicts' (Glasl 1990, p.70 ff.)

3. People do not share their endeavour to acquire knowledge.

We can really only refer to the primacy of individual moral intuitions if we keep working on the cleansing and purification of our perception and thinking, both as individuals

The potential for conflict in communities

and as a community. In that sense building on moral intuition presupposes the material about acquiring knowledge contained in the first part of the *Philosophy of Freedom*. If a community does not seek knowledge in joint endeavour then the moral intuitions can also be flawed. The joint search for knowledge means that every so often the group exchanges its views of customer needs and discusses and examines them, that the images which people have of the way that the community functions are taken seriously and that differences, blind spots, strains and distortions are made the starting point for a closer examination.

4. In the discussion about people's perceptions and their conceptual interpretation people demonstrate too little courage to face the consequences of acquiring knowledge.

When a difference of perception about the way reality is experienced in a community becomes apparent, the courage is often lacking to face up to these differences or contradictions. The result is a false harmony and false tolerance because people do not have the inclination, the time or the courage to get to the bottom of the differences in a debate which will reveal a lot of friction. But if we seek to base ourselves on moral intuitions we have to be prepared to undergo a reciprocal and constructive, if hard, examination. That requires courage. Many communities prefer to accept their differences officially while parading and fighting them in asides and gossip in the corridors. As a rule this leads to a culture of 'cold conflicts' which are the enemy of every open search for the truth.

5. Idealism leads to the establishment of social organisations which assume a higher moral maturity among their members than can be lived in the community at the present time.

This creates a permanent situation where, with the best of moral intentions, too much is asked of those involved. But we cannot – metaphorically speaking – walk on tip-toes indefinitely in order to reach ambitious targets. The decisive element is the degree of mutual dependence created by the rules and structures of a community. The more people are dependent on one another, the more 'brotherliness' and 'sisterliness' as well as awareness and tolerance is required of them. Ethical overloading always occurs where the social structures of a community demand far greater comradeship than people are able to sustain in the long run. Then mutual disappointment mounts up and undermines reciprocal trust. The mood of 'positive effusiveness' at the beginning, which consisted of the idealisation of one another, is transformed into an attitude of 'negative effusiveness' which leads to mutual rejection and in the long term to conflict.

A developmental principle of communities which want to embark on the path of social development should therefore be: The degree of mutual dependence should only be marginally greater than the attitude of open encounter which the members are able to sustain.

Some alternative working communities operate on the principle of income based on need because they consider salary grades to be incompatible with ethical individualism. But this can only work if people accept the different expenditure levels and consumer habits of the individual members without sitting in moral judgement. That presupposes a high degree of tolerance. If there is more than enough money in a community to pay incomes, then there

Free morality assumes maturity

need not be conflict. But if the financial resources are tight and a large withdrawal by one person from the common kitty means that the others are forced to be more modest in their requirements, then a high degree of mutual dependence is created. In such situations anger sets in about colleagues who 'misuse our joint finances as a self-service shop' while others restrict themselves in consideration of the community. Conflict is not far behind. It results from the tension between the moral standards which are demanded and the real moral maturity which a community can live in the course of its social development.

Free morality assumes maturity

So far, I have presented the fundamental ideas of Steiner's 'ethical individualism' as the direction in which I have developed my work in the social sphere because in my view it builds on a solid epistemological basis. Today a number of enterprises, hospitals and therapeutic centres, schools and curative education institutions orientate themselves by these ideas. But the fact that they are endeavouring to implement them does not mean by a long chalk that a community can switch over to 'free morality' from one day to the next. To have seen the value of an idea does not, unfortunately, mean that we can live it straight away either as individuals or as a community. For just as an individual has to embark on a path of exercise and learning in order to be able to improvise freely on a musical instrument while still creating music, a community also has to see itself as a learning community (Geissler 1994). A community can be working continuously towards the goal of creating together the right conditions in the organisation for the development of moral intuitions by all its members and yet it can reach the realistic conclusion that it has only succeeded in doing so here and there. But even if its current practice falls far short of the ideal, that does not invalidate the purpose of its endeavours. A community merely has to be modest enough to admit where it is not yet capable of fulfilling its aims and what the consequences of that are for the development of the organisation. For a major potential for conflict is created when communities want to take the third step in their development before the second one. People then experience their inadequacies and failures and begin to search for scapegoats to blame.

Here we have a key point in Steiner's thinking about moral action. In the course of development, we must aim to acquire the faculty of free morality through exercise and learning. And that means that in the stages along the way we must certainly together create binding norms which do not yet allow unlimited freedom for the existence of individual moral intuitions.

Rudolf Steiner sums it up in the following sentences (p.142): 'The standpoint of free morality, then, does not declare the free spirit to be the only form in which a human being can exist. It sees in the free spirit only the last stage of the human being's evolution. This is not to deny that conduct according to norms has its justification as one stage in evolution.'

Do these words, then, make everything relative once again which was said previously about 'ethical individualism'? No, there are quite clear points of reference for the developmental stages and degrees of maturity of working communities. Bernard Lievegoed and I published the book *Dynamische Unternehmensentwicklung* on this subject in 1993, which describes the four phases in the evolution of all types of social organisations. A brief summary of their main characteristics has been presented in the other chapter in the present book so I will only indicate at this point the significance of the four phases in the evolution of an enterprise for the development towards 'free morality'.

1. The pioneer phase of a community is introduced through the charismatic and socially structuring power of the founder of the enterprise, a development which is subsequently carried on by key individuals in the style of the pioneering phase – under certain circumstances over several generations.

Free morality assumes maturity

By their example these key personalities act as moral authorities because their moral intuitions are lived out by them. The staff in the pioneering phase identify with this moral authority and imitate it in their own actions. Enthusiasm is activated through their feelings and emotions; the charisma of the pioneering personality works through these into the imaginative life and the will of the people in the organisation. They take on responsibility from a feeling of personal connection with the pioneering individual.

The ethic which the key individual lives by example is internalised by the other people – the community is built around these values. Furthermore, the community acquires the ability during this phase to see and grasp the tasks and the organisation through the eyes of the pioneering individual.

2. The differentiated phase of an organisation is built on rational thinking as an ordering and steering force. The personal character as well as the arbitrariness are removed from the aims, objectives and values of the community and the latter characteristics are turned into 'objectified' norms – like the laws of Moses which simply constitute laws and prohibitions.

Through its orientation towards a factual and ordered basis, the differentiated phase brings about a necessary externalisation of morality: Aims, principles and norms have to be comprehensible to everyone on a reasonable and reasoned basis. Thus the organisation acquires the ability to objectify perception and thinking because aims and objectives, norms and rules of the game have to be accessible to reason. The capacity for identification and closeness of the pioneer phase is thus supplemented by the capacity for creating distance and taking an overview of the community. People are enabled to live out their responsibility not from personal loyalty to the pioneer or founder, but because of their understanding of the objective requirements.

3. The integrated phase can continue to build on the lessons of the two preceding phases by creating the conditions which allow people to find and develop the aims and purpose, principles and values for their actions in mutual dialogue. The continuous effort of as many people as possible in the organisation to grasp the needs and requirements of customers or clients allows them to search together and awakens moral intuition. Discussion in teams results in binding agreements about aims and principles of action.

The *internalisation* of a moral orientation in the pioneer phase and the *externalisation* of general norms and rules in the differentiated phase are *brought into equilibrium in dynamic polarised tension* in the individual and joint process of search and clarification. I often use the symbol of the lemniscate, the figure of eight, which represents the rhythmical pulse beat between inner and outer.

4. The associative phase brings with it a fundamental expansion of the awareness and responsibility horizon of the organisation and its people. Aims and objectives rise above the organisation because enterprises cooperate intensively and create many different forms of association (Womack, Jones, Roos 1991, Womack, Jones 1994). They put themselves and their abilities in the service of the general flow of value creation which in the production of goods passes through many organisations from raw material exploitation to the disposal of waste products. This creates an expansion of the awareness and responsibility horizon to a global level because the streams of value creation might start

Free morality assumes maturity

in a mine in Alaska and end, via parts suppliers on several continents, somewhere in China with recycling. The aim of such an expanded horizon is to grasp connections and mutual dependencies and to work on their common consequences. By this means every participating enterprise has to learn to expand the polarity of inner and outer to include a further transformation to create a dynamic equilibrium between inner and outer, between one's own enterprise and the 'company biotope'. (The 'company biotope' comprises all the independent enterprises associated with the flow of value creation.) This method of organisation and management means that value creation as a whole does not lead to the waste and destruction of available resources and potentials but to the development and use of given capacities in the interest of the benefit which the enterprises create jointly.

I have to keep emphasising that this concept of the associative phase is not the dream of an unworldly idealist but is already being implemented by many enterprises (see Glasl, Brugger 1994). Against the background of Rudolf Steiner's statements about the 'reality of freedom' we can thus see that the evolutionary path to the associative phase can lead to an expansion of the wider organisational context. These make possible the development of moral intuition in the sense of 'free morality' in much larger contexts as well. We only have to remember that this is a gradual development which cannot be forced.

The way through the labyrinth

Again and again, social currents appear which are all in favour of peaceful co-existence among nations. But they see the way to achieving this through constructing models or social blueprints backed up by social compulsion. This leads to total outside control and the totalitarian organisation of society which leaves little room for the individual. Such control may be imposed because of the fear of the anti-social drives in people. One hundred years ago already Rudolf Steiner showed in his *Philosophy of Freedom* that the consistent acknowledgement of the spiritual reality in each human being provides the basis for understanding the human capacity for knowledge. And this capacity for knowledge also forms the basis for ethical action which can increasingly develop into activity which is free and based on personal responsibility. I have also tried to show where a different understanding of knowledge leads, as is the case with the modern epistemological school of constructivism. In my judgement, it merely entangles human beings solipsistically within themselves and their physical and material reality. Another consequence of basing one's actions in the world on constructivism is that it can lead to a great ego trip, as I showed in the approach taken by Gerd Gerken which creates the danger of immeasurable over-estimation of one's abilities.

At the start of the twentieth century Rudolf Steiner presented the vision of an associative economy. In order to implement this vision we need fundamentally new structures and institutions. Business itself will have to become active to find and test such forms. It also means that new paths will have to be trodden in the spiritual and cultural life of our society, as well as in the political sphere.

I recognise that this is a long and difficult path fraught with conflict. But the signs of the times indicate that progress is moving in this direction. Throughout the world we see emancipatory movements which, through the ups and downs of events, do in the longer term lead to a rejection of childlike treatment and exploitation. This is a path which leads to freedom and responsibility. If people fight for their freedoms there is inevitably also the danger of egocentric anarchy. Freedom certainly dissolves inhuman forms of society but in itself it does not yet create conditions for social co-existence in accordance with human dignity. The capacity for love as a socially active force is also needed for that.

Then what Rudolf Steiner describes as love of action applies (p. 135-136):

'I ask no person and no rule, "Shall I perform this action?" – but carry it out as soon as I have grasped the idea of it. This alone makes it *my* action. (...) I acknowledge no external principle for my action, because I have found in myself the ground for my action, namely, my love for the action. I do not work out mentally whether my action is good or bad; I carry it out because I *love* it. My action will be "good" if my intuition, steeped in love, finds its right place within the intuitively experienceable world continuum; it will be "bad" if this is not the case.'

The path into a better world is never a straight line but leads through a labyrinth. But just as Theseus in his time was given a red thread by Ariadne before entering the labyrinth, which allowed him to find his way out of the maze again, we need the epistemological certainty of intuition and thinking; an epistemological certainty which represents the linking thread between the individual and the spiritual world. That enables

The way through the labyrinth

us to hold our own in the battle with our own bull-headed Minotaur, whose instincts have risen to his head and who has thus become a prisoner of his own self. We succeed in doing this when we learn to carry responsibility for our own thinking and actions.

References

Biehal, F (Ed.) (1993): *Lean Service,* Bern / Vienna 1993.

Bockemühl, J (1973): 'Vom Lesen im Buch der Natur am Beispiel des Klatschmohns'. In: *(Zeitschrift) Elemente der Naturwissenschaft,* 1/1973.

Geissler, H (1994): *Grundlagen des Organisationslernens,* Weinheim.

Gerken, G (1991): 'Evolution goes to Business'. In: *Gerken Zukunft, Radar für Trends Info-System* 4-5/1991, Worpswerde.

Glasl, F (1975): 'Selbstdiagnose einer Schule'. In: F. Glasl / L. de la Houssaye: *Organisationsentwicklung.* P. Haupt Verlag / Verlag Freies Geistesleben Bern/Stuttgart, p. 107-120.

F. Glasl / L. de la Houssaye: *Organisationsentwicklung,* Haupt / Freies Geistesleben Bern / Stuttgart.

Glasl, F (1975): 'Zwänge zu einem neuen Managementdenken?' In: *GDI-Topics, Brennpunkte* 1/1975, p.103-116.

Glasl, F (Ed.) (1983): *Verwaltungsreform durch Organisationsentwicklung.* Bern / Stuttgart.

Glasl, F (1990): Konfliktmanagement. Ein Handbuch für Führungskräfte und Berater. Haupt / Freies Geistesleben, Bern / Stuttgart.

Glasl, F (1992): 'Die großen Konflikte der Gegenwart und ihre Auswirkungen auf die Unternehmen.' In: A. Dermuth (Ed.),

Imageprofile '92. Konfliktmanagement und Umweltstrategien.
Düsseldorf etc.

Glasl, F / B. Lievegoed (1993): *Dynamische Unternehmensentwicklung. Wie Pionierbetriebe und Bürokratien zu Schlanken Unternehmen werden.* Haupt / Freies Geistesleben Bern/Stuttgart.

Glasl F. / E. Brugger (Ed.) (1994): *Der Erfolgskurs Schlanker Unternehmen. Impulstexte und Praxisbeispiele. Vienna / Bern / Stuttgart.*

Lievegoed, B (1974): *Organisationen im Wandel.* Bern / Stuttgart. English translation published as *The Developing Organisation,* Tavistock, London 1974 and republished by Blackwells, Oxford in 1990.

Lovelock, J (1991): Das Gaia-Prinzip: Die Biographie unseres Planeten. Zürich / Munich, from the English, *The Ages of Gaia: A Bioplan of our Living Earth,* W.W.Norton, (1988), New York

Maturana, H (1988): 'Ontology of Observing: Biological Foundations of Self Consciousness and the Physical Domain of Existence.' In: *Conference Workbook for 'Texts in Cybernetic Theory',* American Society for Cybernetics, Felton, California, October 18-23. See also Morgan G, (1986) *Images of Organisations,* Sage, p235

Maturana, H / F. Varela (1987): *Der Baum der Erkenntnis. Die biologischen Wurzeln des menschlichen Erkennens.* Bern / Munich. Translated from English, *The Tree of Knowledge: The Biological Roots of Human Understanding* (1988) Shambala, Boston.

References

Popper, K (1957): *The Open Society and its Enemies.* Vol I and II.

Schmid, G (1989): 'Die wirklichkeitskonstruktive Perspektive – Systemisches Denken und Professionalität morgen.' In: *Zeitschrift Organisationsentwicklung.* Issue 2 8/1989: 49-65.

Simon, F (Ed.) (1988): *Lebende Systeme.* Berlin / Heidelberg / New York / London / Paris / Tokyo.

Steiner, R: *The Philosophy of Freedom.* Translated by Michael Wilson. London, 1972.

Steiner, R (1915): 'Gemeinsamkeit über uns – Christus in uns.' A lecture, Düsseldorf, 15 June 1915. Dornach 1980.

Varela, F (1994): 'Das Gehirn funktioniert wie eine Jazz-Band.' Interview in: *Der Standard* (Vienna), 21 June 1994.

Womack, J / Jones D. / Roos D. (1990):*The Machine that changed the World,* Rawson Macmillan, New York.

Womack, J / D. Jones (1994): 'From Lean Production to the Lean Enterprise.' In: *Harvard Business Review,* Issue 3/1994, p.84ff.

Other books from Hawthorn Press

Workways: Seven stars to steer by
A path for renewal and inspiration in work
Biography workbook for building an enterprising life
Kees Locher and Jos van der Brug

A jobshift is happening with the end of jobs for life, rapid technical change, the removal of career ladders and the rise of temporary work. Retraining, career changes and lifelong learning are vital for employability. The challenge is to find your own 'work way'. But how?

Workways helps build an enterprising life, by showing you how to:

- **Find your stars to steer by,** through exploring the work questions that matter to you
- **Build your vision for your work,** so as to clarify your direction
- **Focus your energy and get going,** using the stepping stones of helpful tasks
- **Discover your sources of inspiration,** which lead to personal renewal
- **Deepen insight into your life,** by reflecting on the background reading
- **Feel creatively engaged** through artistic exercises and conversations
- **Learn useful skills** such as taking initiatives, reflective learning by doing and feedback
- **Prepare for and take the next step in your working life**

Enterprise of the future

People using **Workways** say:
'*I can now make more conscious choices...*' '*It woke me up...*' '*More confidence and initiative...*' '*Very practical...*' '*Now I can find a better balance in my life...*' '*Now I know my next step...*' '*Helps me re-orientate my working life on a deeper level.*'

The contents of *Workways* include:

7 questions – What matters to me? Where am I? What made me what I am? Who am I? What do I want? What am I going to do? I learn by doing.
There are 37 Tasks, 19 Tips for skills, 19 Explanations, 5 Creative Support Exercises, a Personal Logbook for reflection, diagrams. Part II, *Backgrounds*, includes the biography of Cézanne illustrated with colour pictures.

The 352 page Workbook is A4 size. Advice on how to use the book is given for individuals and self help groups.

The authors Jos van der Brug and Kees Locher have worked for many years as coaches, mentors and as biography counsellors with the **NPI**-Institute for Organisation Development. *Workways* is their unique, accessible and comprehensive guide at a time of jobshift.

Workways provides a mentor within covers for people. wishing to deepen their sense of living their destiny. It also offers a splendid range of tools for mentors to help others... This book has touched me and enriched my life.
    David Megginson, Chair, European Mentoring Centre

I believe that this book will become the fundamental resource book for all mentors, facilitators and HR specialists.
    Dame Rennie Fritchee D.B.E., Chair of Creative Leadership, University of York

Publication date: 1st Sept 1997; 297 x 210mm; 352pp;
Sewn paperback, colour cover; Colour and b/w illustrations;
ISBN 1 869 890 89 2

Other books from Hawthorn Press

The Enterprise of the Future:
Moral intuition in leadership and organisational development
Friedrich Glasl

Friedrich Glasl describes the future of the modern organisation as a unique challenge for personal development. Every organisation, whether a business, a school, a hospital or a voluntary organisation, will have to develop closer relationships with the key stakeholders in its environment – its suppliers, customers, investors and local communities. Our consciousness as managers needs to expand beyond the boundaries of the organisation to work associatively with the community of enterprises with whom we 'share a destiny'.

216 x 138mm; 160pp; Social Ecology series; ISBN 1 869 890 79 5

Eye of the needle:
His life and working encounter with anthroposophy
Bernard Lievegoed

A man of wide ranging interests, Lievegoed combined his profound inner, spiritual research with his pioneering social, medical, educational and management work to produce a number of fascinating books. *The Eye of the Needle* illustrates the dynamics between the inner and outer worlds – and of Lievegoed's ability to work with these dynamics.

216 x 138mm; 103pp; paperback; Social Ecology series; ISBN 1 869 890 50 7

In place of the self:
How drugs work
Ron Dunselman

Why are heroin, alcohol, hashish, ecstasy, LSD and tobacco attractive substances for so many people? Why are unusual, visionary and 'high' experiences so important to users? How can we understand such experiences? These and others questions about drugs and drug use are answered comprehensively in this remarkable book by Ron Dunselman.

216 x 138mm; 304pp; hardback; Social Ecology series;
ISBN 1 869 890 72 8

More precious than light:
How dialogue can transform relationships and build commuity
Margreet van den Brink

Profound changes are taking place as people awaken to the experience of the Christ in themselves. The author is a social consultant and counsellor and offers helpful insights into building relationships. She shows how true encounter can be fostered.

216 x 138mm; 160pp; colour cover; Social Ecology series;
ISBN 1 869 890 83 3

Other books from Hawthorn Press

New eyes for plants:
A workbook for observing and drawing plants
Margaret Colquhoun and Axel Ewald

Here are fresh ways of seeing and understanding nature with a vivid journey through the seasons. Detailed facts are interwoven with artistic insights. Readers are helped by simple observation exercises, by inspiring illustrations which make a companion guide to plant growth around the year. This shows how science can be practised as an art, and how art can help science through using the holistic approach of Goethe. A wide variety of plants are beautifully drawn, from seed and bud to flower and fruit. The drawings are accompanied by helpful suggestions which encourage readers to try out the observation and drawing exercises.
Dr Margaret Colquhoun researches into plants and landscape. Axel Ewald is a sculptor. The book is the outcome of their teaching and research work.

270 x 210mm; 208pp; paperback; colour cover; black and white illustrations. Social Ecology series; ISBN 1 869 890 85 x

Sing me the Creation
Paul Matthews

This is an inspirational workbook of creative writing exercises for poets and teachers. It provides over 300 exercises for improving writing skills and developing the life of the imagination. Although these exercises are intended for group work with adults, teachers will find them easily adaptable to the classroom.
Paul Matthews, a poet himself, taught creative writing at Emerson College, Sussex.

238 x 135; 226pp; paperback; Learning Resources and Rudolf Steiner Education series; ISBN 1 869 890 60 4

Tapestries
Betty Staley

Tapestries gives a moving and wise guide to women's life phases. Drawing on original biographies of a wide variety of women, informed by personal experience and by her understanding of athroposophy, Betty Staley offers a vivid account of life journeys. This book helps readers reflect on their own lives and prepare for the next step in weaving their own biographical tapestry. This will be published in Summer 1997 in the Biography and Self-Development series.

A companion book to *Tapestries* will chart the twelve senses, the four temperament, the twelve philosophical viewpoints and soul types. To be published in Autumn 1997

Tools for transformation:
A personal study
Adam Curle

This exploration of mediation, development and education draws on case studies from disparate cultural and geographical sources, reminding us of our participative relationship with the fabric of life. Specific issues include approaches to violence, negotiation, the nature of democracy, consensus management, community development, non-violence and learning for life.

210 x 138mm; 224pp; sewn limp bound; Conflict and Peacemaking series; ISBN 1 869 890 21 3

Other books from Hawthorn Press

Vision in action
Chrisopher Schaefer and Tÿno Voors

This well thought-out book breathes life into the worn-out concept of vision. One finds in it an enlivening imagination of how to develop new initiatives. Like all worthwhile advice, it is based on hard-won life experience. Work with this book and you will find real help in developing small organizations.
Robert Michael Burnside, Director, Organization Development Products, Center for Creative Leadership

This book is excellent – a well-written exposition of organizational development and the problems that groups tend to encounter as they progress. I highly recommend it to anyone in the field.
Caroline Estes, Co-Founder of Alpha Farm and Master Facilitator

Vision in Action *explores and facilitates the vital process of social innovation.*
Hazel Henderson, author of Building a Win-Win World: Life Beyond Economic Warfare

This is a very helpful book, full of examples, exercise, and case studies. The last section, Signs of Hope, describes many wonderful ways in which we are indeed creating a better world. Read it!
Rachael Flug, CEO, Diaperwraps, Inc.

Socially-oriented initiatives and small organizations play a vital role in a healthy, evolving society. Vision in Action *offers important and practical perspectives that capture this essence.*
Will Brinton, President of Woods End Laboratory

Many readers will find Vision *a valuable source of inspiration and help.*
James Robertson

115

Enterprise of the future

Vision in Action is a workbook for those involved in social creation – in collaborative deeds that can influence the social environment in which we live and where our ideas and actions can matter.

This is a user-friendly, hands-on guide for developing healthy small organizations – organizations with soul and spirit.

Chapters include:
    Starting Initiatives;
    Getting Going;
    Ways of Working Together;
    Funding Initiatives;
    Vision, Mission, and Long-Range Planning;
    Fund-raising.

235 x 145mm; 256pp; paperback; Social Ecology series;
ISBN 1 869 890 88 4

Orders

If you have difficulties ordering from a bookshop, you can order direct from:
>Hawthorn Press,
>1 Lansdown Lane,
>Stroud,
>Gloucestershire, GL5 1BJ

Fax: (01453) 751138   Telephone: (01453) 757040

Hawthorn Press' Social Ecology Series is available in North America from:
>Anthroposophic Press,
>3390 Route 9,
>Hudson,
>NY 12534

Fax:(518) 851 2047   Telephone:(518) 851 2054

Anthroposophic Press' Spirituality and Social Renewal Series is closely linked, and includes such titles as:

H. Zimmerman, *Speaking, Listening, Understanding – The Art of Creating Conscious Conversation*